Capture at Arnhem

Other Military Memoirs published by the Windrush Press

The Recollections of Rifleman Harris
    Edited and Introduced by Christopher Hibbert
The Letters of Private Wheeler
    Edited and with a Foreword by B H Liddell Hart
The Diaries of a Napoleonic Footsoldier
    Edited and Introduced by Marc Raeff
A Soldier of the 71st
    Edited and Introduced by Christopher Hibbert
The Wheatley Diary
    Edited and Introduced by Christopher Hibbert
The Recollections of Sergeant Morris
    Edited by John Selby with an Introduction by Peter Young
Letters Home from the Crimea
    Edited by Philip Warner

Titles in the GREAT BATTLES series

Agincourt by Christopher Hibbert
Hastings by Peter Poyntz Wright
Edgehill: 1642 by Peter Young
Marston Moor: 1644 by Peter Young
The Boyne and Aughrim by John Kinross
Corunna by Christopher Hibbert
Wellington's Peninsular Victories by Michael Glover
Trafalgar: The Nelson Touch by David Howarth
Borodino by Digby Smith
Waterloo: A Near Run Thing by David Howarth
The Eastern Front 1914–18: Suicide of the Empires by Alan Clark
Arnhem by Christopher Hibbert

Also

The Great Civil War
    by Alfred H Burne and Peter Young

Capture at Arnhem

CAPTAIN HARRY ROBERTS

THE WINDRUSH PRESS · GLOUCESTERSHIRE

First published in Great Britain by
The Windrush Press in 1999
Little Window, High Street,
Moreton-in-Marsh
Gloucestershire GL56 0LL
Tel: 01608 652012
Fax: 01608 652125
Email: *windrush@windrushpress.com*
Website: www.windrushpress.com

Copyright © Muriel Roberts 1999

The right of Muriel Roberts to be identified as copyright holder of this work has been asserted by her in accordance with the Copyright, Designs and Patents Act 1988

ALL RIGHTS RESERVED
British Library in Cataloguing Data
A catalogue record for this book is available from the British Library

ISBN 1 900624 27 3

Typeset by Archetype IT Ltd, website http://www.archetype-it.com
Printed and bound in Malta by Interprint Ltd., Malta

The Front cover picture shows: A photograph of the author in front of a painting of Stirlings and Horsas by John Bryce GAvA by kind permission of the artist and the Guild of Aviation Artists.

Cover design by Sandy Field

To order your free Windrush Press catalogue featuring military titles, plus travel books, general history and other titles, please phone us on
01608 652012 or **01608 652025**
Fax us on **01608 652125** Email: **Windrush@windrushpress.com**
Website: **www.windrushpress.com**
Or write to:
The Windrush Press Limited
Little Window, High Street, Moreton-in-Marsh
Gloucestershire, GL56 0LL, UK

DEDICATION

This book is dedicated to all my old comrades in REME with whom I had the honour to serve, and who did not live to see our victory.

Especially my workshop troops in 6th Guards Tank Brigade Workshop, who were killed by a flying bomb in England shortly after my departure and, of course, those men who flew in with me to 'A Bridge too Far' at Arnhem on 18 September 1944.

H.R.

Acknowledgement

My grateful thanks to Professor Cyril Wilson, of the Shrivenham Military College, for his help and encouragement in having this book of my husband's work published.

Muriel Roberts
February 1999

The author, Captain Harry Roberts, showing REME flashes Para Wings. This was taken on 1 August 1944, six weeks before Arnhem

Contents

Foreword
  by Major General Michael J H Walsh CB, CBE, DSO, DL   viii
List of Photographs and Maps   x
Author's Service Record   xii

CHAPTER 1 Training for Combat   1

CHAPTER 2 The Battle of Arnhem   21

CHAPTER 3 Prisoner of War   39

CHAPTER 4 Oflag IX A/Z   65

CHAPTER 5 The Outside World   88

CHAPTER 6 The March to Freedom   104

CHAPTER 7 The Hazards of Liberty   127

Postscript   140

Afterword   142
The Parachute Regiment and Airborne Forces Prayer   143
Index   145

Foreword

by Major General Michael J H Walsh

CB, CBE, DSO, DL

There have been many books written about the Battle of Arnhem but, to my recollection, little has been told by those who, at the end of that heroic stand at the bridge, the Oosterbeek crossroads and the Hartenstein enclave, were taken prisoners of war. Many of these were suffering from severe gun shot wounds, broken limbs, battle fatigue and exhaustion. Harry Roberts, then a lieutenant in the small Advanced Workshop Detachment REME, 1st Airborne Division, was severely wounded when his glider came to an abrupt halt amongst the German troops defending the Landing Zone.

Harry's story of his survival, his treatment firstly by our own medics in the Casualty Clearing Station at Oosterbeek, then as a prisoner of war at a hospital at Apeldoorn, makes compelling reading. His courage, fortitude and sheer Yorkshire 'grit' to survive, both then and later in various POW camps in Germany, is an example to us all, especially those who belong to the 'Profession of Arms' or who risk their lives in ventures on land or at sea.

I was fortunate to know Harry when he and his wife were living in retirement in the Wiltshire village of Liddington. He was a staunch member of the Swindon Branch of the Parachute Regimental Association. A number of members of this small but active branch also fought at Arnhem.

Harry was born in York, the son of a former sergeant in the KOYLI who fought in France in the First World War. He started his working life, at the age of 16, as a fitter in the old LNER

Railway Carriage and Wagon Works in York. Despite efforts to join the RAF as an air gunner, blocked by his employers as a 'Reserved Occupation', he eventually volunteered and was accepted in 1943 for a newly formed Corps – the Royal Electrical and Mechanical Engineers, REME.

On being demobbed in 1947, after active service in Palestine, he rejoined the LNER in York, qualifying as a Fellow of the Institute of Mechanical Engineers. Following senior positions in York, Doncaster and Derby he was appointed Works Manager at the former GWR Workshops in Swindon. This was at a difficult time when Dr Beeching's wide sweeping reforms were devastating regional railway networks. His personal leadership and determination, shown so clearly in this book, once more came to the fore. There are many former railwaymen and engineers in Swindon today who are grateful for his efforts on their behalf.

They, together with his old comrades in Airborne Forces, particularly those who fought at Arnhem, will be grateful to his widow, Muriel, for her resolution to have Harry's story published.

List of Photographs and Maps

Frontispiece: The author, Captain Harry Roberts showing REME flashes Para Wings. This was taken on 1 August 1944, six weeks before Arnhem

The vehicle waterproofing tests	6
A REME transporting trailer	6
1st Airborne Division October 1945 REME	18
Map of wartime Europe and the location of Arnhem	22
Dropping Zones near Wolfheze station (Photo: MOD)	25
Hotel Vreewijk at Oosterbeek crossroads	31
A map of Arnhem and surrounding area	34
The Hartenstein Hotel, Oosterbeek	36
Typical damage caused at the Battle of Arnhem in the Oosterbeek area (Photo: GH Maassen)	37
Specimen pages from author's diary with transcription	40
The author's POW Identity Card	52
The family photographs that were confiscated by the Germans	66
The Kriegie cooker used by POWs	78

x

POW entertainment	80
POW camp radio	82
1944 Christmas card from Oflag IX A/Z	86
Homemade POW tools	95
A map of the forced march	106
The last day in Germany at Wimmelburg	134
Eisenstadt: Taken with a 'liberated' camera showing the POWs at the airfield	136
Real girls in Brussels	138

Author's Service Record

Enlisted REME	February 1943
Posted to 165 officer training unit	April 1943
Commissioned REME	June 1943
Posted to 101 Company	June 1943
Posted to 6th Guards Tank Brigade Workshops	November 1943
Posted to 4th Battalion Grenadier Guards	December 1943
Posted to 1st Airborne Division	February 1944
Arnhem and POW	September 1944–April 1945
Posted to 1st Airborne Division	August 1945
Posted to HQ 1st Para Brigade	September 1945
Posted to Palestine	March 1946
Returned to UK	December 1946
Posted to 156 Transit Camp	December 1946
Released from Army service	June 1946

CHAPTER 1

Training for Combat

(Recollections of 1st Airborne
Division Workshops REME)

The formation of Airborne Division Workshops REME (Royal Electrical and Mechanical Engineering Corps) in 1943 must have virtually coincided with the formation of REME itself, because REME volunteers in the UK found that an advance party had already left for the Airborne Division in the Middle East, when they joined the base unit at Andover in March 1943.

All REME Airborne troops were committed to travel by glider into battle, but specialists, who could be required to parachute into action, were selected from trained volunteers within the unit.

Major Jack Carrick was OC Workshops from 26 February 1943, with Captain George Deadman as his second-in-command. Both these officers had long distinguished careers with the unit, Jack seeing it through to disbandment in late 1945, and George only leaving it to take command of his own unit just prior to this date. Captain Hal Snow, who was the only other surviving officer from 1st Airborne on the group photograph taken in October 1945, was with the unit in North Africa, joining them on 7 May 1943. Perhaps I am mistaken, but I seem to remember that he was a Regimental Officer attached to REME, rather than an EME, certainly he never undertook any technical duties.

The 1st Airborne Division consisted of three brigades with the 1st Parachute Brigade under the command of Brigadier Gerald Lathbury; this brigade was formed in the UK and had already experienced airborne warfare. The 4th Parachute Brigade was recruited by Brigadier 'Shan' Hackett from Middle East veterans, and comprised 156, 10 and 11 Parachute Battalions. The 3rd Brigade was an Air Landing Unit, i.e. glider-borne, comprising the 1st Border Regiment, the 7th KOSB and the 2nd South Staffords, under the command of Brigadier 'Pip' Hicks, again consisting mostly of seasoned veterans.

Each brigade was a self-contained unit with Divisional troops providing full back-up resources, including REME workshops. In early 1943, these workshops were located near Mascara in Algeria, where they received their first 'battle orders' – each man had to kill a minimum of twenty flies a day – to minimise the dysentery which was sweeping through all ranks. The workshops had been located in a horse stud farm!

Later in 1943, the workshops moved from Mascara to M'Saken, near Sousse in Tunisia, and this is where the founder members of Airborne REME did their parachute and glider training. Major Carrick experienced a very intimate contact with a large cactus bush during his parachute training, an incident he was never allowed to forget. The first glider training also took place near to this location with American glider pilots. The fact that the pilots wore parachutes, whilst our men had to rely on them to get them down safely, was not exactly conducive to confidence. Glider-borne troops received one shilling a day extra pay and the parachutists two shillings a day – in modern parlance, 5p and 10p, respectively, so airborne volunteers were hardly in it for the extra money.

During their sojourn in North Africa, in addition to their normal divisional commitments, the workshops did a lot of work for the Long Range Desert Group, the SAS and 'Popsky's' Private Army, adapting and disguising their vehicles, many of which had been illegally acquired, with extra fuel and water tanks, special gun and mortar mountings, etc. General Montgomery's personal support for the special forces was not always shared by his desk-bound subordinates, so the former used their own initiative to equip themselves for their specialised roles.

The close association between the Division and these special forces induced an *esprit-de-corps* in 1st Airborne, which I found quite unique. The 6th Airborne Division, in which I served later in my career, had a very proud battle history, but it was not comparable to the 1st, and I missed the confident egoistical comradeship enjoyed by all ranks in 1st Airborne Division. Officers all had pet names which troops used amongst themselves. It was never General Hopkinson, it was always 'Hoppy' – he was killed in Italy – and the three Brigadiers were Gerald, Pip and Shan. This went right through the officer corps, and the respect which our heterogeneous collection of troops afforded their officers was earned by the fact that, right from the top, officers led from the front – a tradition still being followed judging by the parachute commissioned and non-commissioned casualty lists in the Falklands War.

Our CO Major Carrick was no exception to this rule, and demanded a high standard from his officers. Some officers like Captain 'Dizzy' Dunlop, who left to join either the SAS or LRDG, I am not sure which, left with Jack's blessing, others with the toe of his boot.

Jack Carrick understood his men better than most officers and the stories about him are endless. He was the most hirsute man I ever saw; one day he was sitting on the open-air bogs, no shirt on and his trousers around his knees, when a newcomer to the unit asked him, not too politely, what time it was. Getting no response from Jack, he said, 'Hey, you hairy bugger, what time is it?' Jack politely told him; the man's face when he saw Jack later on, was a picture. Silence was far more effective than any official reprimand.

Following the cessation of hostilities in North Africa, which had resulted in very heavy casualties to the Para battalions, the Division led the invasion of Sicily but REME involvement was limited to specialist armourers, etc. The main workshop party went across to the subsequent invasion of Italy by sea, where they remained until the Division was recalled to the UK in December 1943, to prepare for the invasion of Europe. Jack Carrick and George Deadman brought back two Guzzi motorbikes which were their pride and joy. Unfortunately, there were no spares and the maintenance of these bikes became a particular nightmare for my Motor Transport Section.

Another perennial problem was maintaining the three Brigadiers' Humber staff cars to a 100 mph capability so that they could race each other – or so my man informed me! I nearly lost my job through one of them, because his car was always in trouble; nothing we did seemed to make it better. Fortunately, I came across him one day just after he had broken down again, and, automatically ran into a barrage of abuse. I had found the answer to this problem very quickly because there had not been enough time for his driver to remove the evidence. Vehicle antifreeze was not in common use at this period in time, and drivers had to drain off the water from the radiator and cylinder block each night. On the following morning it was necessary to close the drain cocks, which were not very conveniently situated, and refill with water. This particular driver was using aircraft antifreeze to save himself this rather irksome task.

I am afraid that my initial response to the Brigadier was delivered in the same dumb insolent tones which I had learned, by bitter experience, from the RSM of my previous Guards battalion. Fortunately for me, he must have recalled his own unwarranted accusations of a few minutes earlier and he accepted my 'reproaches' in good grace.

Our UK workshop was located at Sleaford in Lincolnshire and enjoyed good facilities. The Officers' Mess was in an isolated house – I think on the Lincoln road – with the main camp in Boston road. This had been purpose-built as an army depot and was very comfortable by wartime standards. My motor transport workshops were in a substantial building which, originally, could have been an agricultural warehouse, or tractor depot, with its own enclosed yard sited adjacent to the railway station. Other workshop sections were spread throughout the town, so we were completely integrated with the cinema, shops, dance hall, public houses and other facilities beneficial to troops' welfare.

The officer establishment in February 1944, when I joined the 1st Airborne Division was as follows:

Major Jack Carrick	OC Unit, bachelor, home town York.
Captain George Deadman	Second-in-Command, married to WAAF officer.
Captain Hal Snow	Regimental Officer, bachelor, home town Edinburgh.
Lieutenant Geoff Manning	Wireless, instruments & armourers, bachelor, home town Leicester.
Lieutenant Harry Roberts	Motor transport & Bren carriers, bachelor, home town York (Author of this memoir).

Other REME officers in the Division were:

Lieutenant Colonel Kinvig	Commander REME (CREME)
Captain F W Ewens	Adjutant
Captain R Hayward	EME Royal Artillery
Captain W E Titmus	EME Telecommunications
Captain E G Newby	EME 1st Air Landing Brigade
Lieutenant A M Brodie	Workshop Officer, attached to HQ 4th Parachute Brigade commanding its LAD

Jack Carrick certainly believed in intensive training. I had joined the unit on 10 February 1944, and, in less than a fortnight was on a camouflage course in Norwich. Immediately this was completed I went straight on to a 'B' vehicle waterproofing course at Craven Arms. I discovered, much later on, that some contingency plans for 'D' Day involved the Division in a rescue sea-borne landing. Returning to the unit on 5 March, I had a brief reintroduction to my workshop staff whilst training them in waterproofing techniques and holding practical trials.

Jack was not content with the basic vehicle and AFV waterproofing, and we had to improvise ways of transporting our workshop trailers through beach landings, without damaging the contents. Having worked out a successful method of loading them on top of a jeep, it was not long before the Artillery wanted their 75mm howitzers carried in a similar manner. The trials were

The vehicle waterproofing tests

A REME transporting trailer

so successful that they were photographed for wider circulation, and my copy prints are the only ones I have of the units' activities prior to Arnhem.

The modifications we carried out on jeeps, etc. at the request of different units, would break the heart of a War Office bureaucrat. My tradesmen were a very skilled bunch who had learned how to improvise during their involvement with the special forces in North Africa. One unit 'acquired' a pair of American aircraft air-cooled machine guns with a horrendous rate of fire, which we finally succeeded in mounting on the scuttle of a jeep. It was a firing trial I vividly remember.

There were many colourful characters in the unit, one who comes to mind was a carpenter from a gypsy background. My first experience with him was when he was sent to an ordnance depot, with a properly authorised chit, to collect some timber to carry out modifications to a general's command vehicle. Some petty bureaucrat decided that an Airborne Division was not entitled to material such as this and refused to honour the request. This put me in a quandary, so I told a suitably 'qualified' NCO to acquire the material by whatever means he thought necessary. They acquired it alright; I did not ask how. The modification was completed before the Military Police came around to see if there was any connection between the stores refusing my demand note and someone breaking into the depot and stealing about ten times as much.

It was the sheer volume of pilferage which put them off our trail; if my men had only taken what we actually required, the police enquiries might have been somewhat deeper. Needless to say, my gypsy carpenter was involved in the 'snatch' party.

On another occasion, the whole workshop was lined up in convoy, waiting to take part in Divisional manoeuvres. I was walking down the side doing a last minute check when I heard a goat bleating. Having traced this unusual noise to a three tonner, I was horrified to find three goats in it; Gardiner, my gypsy carpenter, was most indignant – it was not his fault – the order to go on manoeuvres had come too quickly and he had not had sufficient time to sell them at a profit.

This was when I found out that he combined market trading with his military duties! It was too late for me to do anything as the convoy started to move whilst I was still questioning Gardiner, so, we took the goats on manoeuvres. They were all in milk so I was able to provide the unit with this fresh delicacy. My cover story to Jack was received with a straight face, belied by the twinkle in his eye. He encouraged us to use our initiative at all times. Gardiner was no stranger to him; he was probably the most regular discipline case in the unit, noted for the ingenuity and originality of his excuses as to why it had been necessary to overstay his leave. Gardiner was most upset when I refused to pay for the milk, on the grounds that His Majesty's Government was paying for the goats' transport and keep.

We had a love/hate relationship with the Americans at this stage of the war, as, during the invasion of Sicily their towing planes had dropped some of our gliders into the sea to avoid the anti-aircraft fire. REME workshops, not having been involved in this particular fiasco, were more parochially interested in the tools and equipment of our American allies, which were in very short supply in the British Army. Our basic form of transport was the American jeep, and the relevant spanners and other tools were as rare as diamonds. What could not be obtained by legal means required an alternative system; 1st Airborne always was a law unto itself and had in its ranks a very wide cross-section of society.

Myself and one of my staff sergeants were the 'front-line troops' whose success depended on a much larger 'supporting network'. We would arrive at an American base in our jeep, and, bluffing our way past the sentries, I would ask to be directed to their Transport Officer. Once inside, the Yanks were always most obliging, and, when I outlined some of the problems we were experiencing in maintaining their American vehicles, a tour of their workshops was soon forthcoming. All queries were patiently dealt with and I learned a lot in a very short time. Lunch in their Mess was usually quite an experience in itself.

In the meantime, my driver – the staff sergeant – would seek out a suitable 'target' in the stores; he had an unerring instinct for selecting the right man, in the right place. An offer to share a drink of whisky soon led to a straight barter of tools for Scotch whisky. It was a perfect arrangement. I substantially increased the know-how of the unit, the staff sergeant made it the best equipped unit in REME, the American officers enjoyed their sudden popularity with wearers of red berets, and the American sergeants enjoyed their amber nectar. I never enquired where the whisky came from. It certainly never came from our official unit allocation. The real credit must, therefore, go to our 'supporting network'.

My parachute training was completed in April 1944, following which I received instruction in the crating of jeeps and six-pound guns ready for dropping by parachute. Four sixty-foot parachutes were utilised for this purpose and automatically released when the hydraulic 'mushroom rams' under the crates hit the ground. Without this facility the chute would drag the gun or the jeep over the ground and damage them. I was the only person in the Division trained in this skill and, shortly after D-Day on 1 June, I had to put this training into practical use to reinforce the beach head.

At that time, I was on manoeuvres in Wales and had to be relocated and brought back to Tarrant Rushton in a small RAF plane: an occasion I vividly remember. Without thinking, I picked up my RAF-type parachute by means of its 'D' ring: it opened! I had to pay a fine to have it repacked. The parachute wings on my arm only added to my embarrassment.

It was around this time that I experienced another major embarrassment. Because all road signs had been removed so as not to help enemy parachutists, it was the practice to use any member of the unit with local knowledge to guide convoys through towns. Thus, I had to lead a convoy through my home town, York. Having taken the convoy through the small roads into York and right up to a straight road leading out of it, I decided to take the opportunity to visit my fiancée. Unfortunately, the convoy broke in the middle and missed the vehicle which had been in front; the rear half had quite a job keeping up with my motorcycle.

As I greeted my fiancée at her front gate, we suddenly became aware of an interested audience from three-ton lorries, heavy breakdown trucks, Bren gun carriers and jeeps with trailers, which very quickly jammed solid the cul-de-sac in which she lived.

Life was very hectic, the major saw to that. When we were not on stand-to, the major and, either my fellow lieutenant, Geoff Manning or myself were away on a course or out on a training detail. He had a very practical way of 'blooding' his subalterns. We would be sent out on a specific route with an Advanced Workshop Detachment (AWD), and told in what areas to set up our workshops, to a timetable which had to be strictly adhered to. Sometimes he would pay us a surprise visit to check on the adequacy of our defences, etc. but, usually we learned by experience how to cope on hard rations in remote areas of the countryside, to a very tight schedule. Every man in the detachment had automatic tasks to carry out on arrival at each new workshop site. The officer arranged the basic layout, compatible with the topography. A senior NCO organised an initial defence system, another party dug latrines, someone else brewed-up, and a foraging party went out on a recce for example.

The major had us all trained down to the last little detail, with a view to ensuring that the workshop facilities were made operational in an ever-reducing time spiral. We had a major exercise with the full Division in Yorkshire, sleeping rough and living on hard rations. The OC moved our camp every day, just to satisfy himself that every man in the unit knew his role to perfection, and everything ran like well-oiled clockwork.

Major Carrick was a tough, uncompromising dour Yorkshireman, who inspired in his unit a loyalty and devotion which was quite special. Officers, NCOs and men would cheerfully have followed him to hell, confident in the knowledge that he would know the way back.

D-Day arrived and we just could not believe the news; how

anyone could invade Europe without our involvement was just beyond comprehension. The accepted knowledge that 6th Airborne Division had been specifically trained for this task for several months was of little consolation, especially to the two subalterns and twenty-seven men who had been selected for our Advanced Workshop Detachment to go in with the first assault.

D-Day did not see the end of our training; it probably got even more stringent, although we did spend less time away from the unit. The repetitive operational 'stand-tos' necessitated both subalterns being in easy reach. We now concentrated on developing various tools and spares packs, to cover every conceivable type of operation, with minimum weight and volume considerations. The men were trained and retrained, some of the training being potentially more lethal than others.

A typical example of this was, probably, our success in the use of motorcycles and jeeps towing a bevy of troops on folding bicycles at quite a high speed. The technique was quite simple, rather like the gliders; each man clasped a wooden handgrip to his handlebars, which in turn, was attached to the towing unit with parachute cord. Every man, therefore, had his own option when to cast-off. The secret was in the formation layout, because each bicycle had to be well clear of the others, as the sudden deceleration of a cast-off created havoc with the remainder of the men, who could not take evasive action with sixty-pound packs on their backs.

The officers, of course, had to train by example, and I must admit that the wing-nuts holding my folding bicycle together were the most personally inspected piece of equipment I ever looked at. The system worked at Arnhem, although I understand the speeds obtained were relatively slow compared to our UK speed records. However, back to D-Day.

Unbeknown to the rank and file, the role of 1st Airborne Division had been decided a long time before the invasion. We were 'strategic reserves' and were expected to move into action at very short notice, as and when required.

In the three months between D-Day and the final decimation

11

of 1st Airborne at Arnhem, we were briefed for operations, and then stood-down again, no less than sixteen times! The first only involved our 4th Parachute Brigade, who would have dropped on the beaches as emergency back-up, if the invasion started to go wrong. Lieutenant Brodie, who was attached to 4th Brigade, would take in a parastick of four craftsmen and our workshop was supplementing this, with Geoff Manning taking in fourteen more para craftsmen. I drew the short straw and was allocated thirteen men and a glider. Gliders do not normally land on invasion beaches, which meant that we would have to land in the middle of the fighting. That did not bother me as much as the number thirteen which I really thought was tempting providence.

We were on standby from 2 June for about a week before this operation was superseded by the second plan – to use the whole Division for a seaborne landing, in the event of any major crisis arising in the beach head itself.

On 11 June, Monty requested that our Division be dropped at Evrecy, south-west of Caen, behind German lines, in order to assist 7th Armoured Division in their encirclement of German panzers in that area. The planners wanted a night drop but we, naturally, wanted to drop by day. It really is beyond my comprehension how anyone could even think that 10,000 men could regroup in the dark, into their fighting units, in the middle of a raging battle, in strange territory, following a 'run-in' under heavy dispersing Ack-Ack fire.

Air Chief Marshal Leigh-Mallory refused to sanction this operation on the grounds that it would be too expensive, and the Royal Navy could not guarantee to hold their fire when we flew over them: shades of Crete again. The codename 'Wild Oats' was an apt name for this rather naïve operation which was cancelled on 13 June; meanwhile, the thrust of 7th Armoured Division towards Evrecy had failed.

It will be appreciated that life at this time was hectic and consequently, it is difficult to identify which of these early operations was a real suicide effort. This latter operation involved dropping the whole Division in the path of three advancing

Panzer Divisions, which could have pushed the bridgehead back into the sea. Fortunately, for us, Hitler refused to commit them into action against the advice of his generals. If they had started to move forward, our orders were 'to inflict maximum casualties and thus, slow down their threat'. At the briefing someone asked why much of the routine details had been omitted, such as passwords for example. The response was that these were irrelevant: 'how many survivors are you anticipating from one lightly armed Airborne Division against three Panzer Divisions?' made everyone think very deeply.

REME paras and glider troops were to be used simply as fighting troops; we were not even going to carry one spanner! I recall that I would be in a glider, so, utilising its basic load carrying capacity, I made arrangements to commandeer local Home Guard 'Blacker Bombards' and 'sticky' grenades, in the knowledge that the battalions would grab all the plate and other anti-tank missiles in the immediate vicinity. I did not fancy trying to tackle Tiger tanks with rifles, but I had a head and shoulders start with Home Guard anti-tank equipment; I had served as an instructor and was an expert in these weapons.

Geoff and I could not change our picked teams, so, after stand-down from this suicide mission, we regrouped our teams into operational fighting units, and quietly ensured that they all received supplementary military training in specialist tank-busting skills in which they had, unknowingly, been allocated. We did not intend being caught out a second time.

The next operation was targeted on the capture of St Malo in Brittany, airborne from the land side, in conjunction with a sea attack by the navy. However, the navy discovered too many sea-based deterrents to their role, and so, this plan was cancelled. I think the next operation was for us to unite with the Maquis against the German flank, prior to the Americans breaking out of the Cherbourg Peninsula. We were never told why 'Raising Brittany' was cancelled – in any case, we were too busy with its successor, in which we were targeted to capture Vannes at the south of the Loire. This was cancelled, to be followed by 'Sword

Hilt': the Morlaix-Lannion area in north Brittany was its target. It will be no surprise to you to find that this was also cancelled.

'Transfigure' seemed a potentially good operation; in which we would collaborate with the Americans to take Paris. In accordance with the detailed planning, which Jack insisted on for each and every operation, I studied a map of our sector of Paris, and decided on a transport depot located near a major road junction as the best site for my Motor Transport Section. This subsequently caused a certain amount of hilarity, and no one ever believed my reasons for selecting this particular site when it became known that it was next door to one of the most upper-class brothels in Paris. I never did live this one down, especially with my contacts in the various battalions who sincerely thought that REME was broadening the servicing scope of its Advanced Workshop Detachment. Unfortunately, General de Gaulle objected to foreigners liberating Paris and, to our everlasting regret, this operation was cancelled at a very late stage.

Two more operations were based on establishing bridgeheads, one just below Rouen and the other at Les Andelys, and twice we were to be hurled ahead of the advancing Allies in Belgium. Finally, there was 'Comet', in which we were to seize three river crossings in Holland. Tragically, this was cancelled in favour of Operation Market Garden – the ill-fated battle of Arnhem.

The REME role varied in each operation, in some Geoff and I would both parachute in with only a handful of specialists, others involved glider transport with the full AWD. There were one or two operations where we knew that we would be fighting as infantry.

The Division was becoming more and more cynical and disillusioned when it became obvious that we were being used to intimidate the enemy, probably, in some instances, leaking information in order to encourage the Germans to move limited reserves to threatened areas. Also, prior to Arnhem, the airborne forces had been allowed to plan their own landings and tactics at quite low command levels. Now, such decisions were being taken by chairborne experts at Army Headquarters. A typical example of their stupidity was after Arnhem, when some queried why the paras had not been dropped on the open ground next to the bridge instead of having to fight through several miles of suburbs. The classic reply received was 'because the ground was too soft'!

Incidentally, the previous operation, Comet, had been cancelled because the same experts decided that one brigade of around 2,500 men was not adequate to take the bridge by *coup-de-main*. They would put in 5,300 men, obviously forgetting that 3,000 of them were needed to guard the dropping zones for the next day's lift. This left roughly the same number to take the bridge as we had planned. However, instead of actually dropping on the bridge they were now several miles away. With friends like that who needs enemies?

It will be appreciated that the effect of this continuous stream of stand-to and cancellation was not conducive to good morale. It was also becoming obvious that the more senior officers, who were privy to all the behind-the-scenes 'cock-ups', were themselves becoming disillusioned. Loyalty to their troops resulted in hitherto undetected cynicism rising to the surface. Regimental officers had to forget their own misgivings because it was becoming very difficult to maintain units at the required level of fighting efficiency for months on end, without a target in sight.

In the end, the powers that be recognised the danger signs and we were the only units granted weekend leave at the critical stages of the Normandy battles. What could not be achieved by army discipline and all the Military Police in the world, was achieved by the female of the species in one short weekend. Troops went on leave like rampaging lions and returned like shorn sheep.

The fighting units were affected the worst because they were repeatedly keyed-up for action and then let down again. Routine training in between operations could not absorb the mental frustration and reactions. REME was in a much better position; first of all only the AWD, which was a relatively small percentage of the total unit strength, had the mental pressure of imminent action and secondly, and most important, we had our routine work to absorb energies and thoughts. As time went on the road accident rate increased and we were hard pressed to keep up with the repairs. Although I could, and did, delegate a lot of work to my NCOs, I kept picking up other extraneous duties, one of which was police liaison officer.

This arose because of an incident when a key member of my AWD team and his friend got mixed up with some paras who were taking their frustrations out on a bunch of American airmen over the usual cause – the local ladies. This, apparently, had been more violent than usual and the civilian police were reluctant to part with the culprits because of the damage in and around the pub where the fight took place.

It was a stalemate situation when I arrived; the para officer not having made much headway, I outlined to the police the pressures that the men were under, the doubtful wisdom of locking them up, either in a civil or military jail, when their country could be sending them into action any day. Their detention would not repair the damage and the army was all red tape and slow to react. In the meantime, the pub was losing trade. As he could see, I was a REME officer with my own workshop – if the landlord agreed to my proposal, I would personally guarantee that the punishment fitted the crime, and the guilty would not have any free time until they had expunged their offences.

Much to my surprise, the police agreed to my suggestion. I 'borrowed' one of our Military Police to march them out of the police station, in true military style, to the scene of the previous night's affray. It was an impressive display of how the army treats its miscreants, and even the accompanying police constable was moved to sympathy. The landlord and I quickly reached an amicable compromise, substituting additional work for the cost of replacing the glasses, etc. However, when I returned to the police station to report back, I was pressurised to help the paras in a similar arrangement.

It all turned out very successfully; we used the young paras to lop trees, cut grass, dig gardens, etc. for the householders around the pub who were elderly, infirm and grass-widows. It developed from a punishment detail into an adoption society, enjoying, I suspect, a lot of home comforts. From then onwards, however, I found my advocacy role a big drain on my time; it soon became obvious that no one else wanted it and I was stuck with it.

Some time prior to Arnhem, I had volunteered for the SAS (Special Air Service) and had passed with flying colours, after pointing out that an engineer with my technical qualifications could immobilise bridges and equipment, more or less to any planned repair schedule so that the advancing Allies could reinstate such facilities with the minimum effort. My stress diagram of a Warren beam bridge, together with alternative calculated plans of destruction based on required repair times clinched it. The two adjudicators were still reeling from an initial warm-up discourse on railway sabotage techniques. Within a few days of this examination an affirmative response was received: I was on my way to join the SAS.

Simultaneously, Market Garden came to life. From what I could gather, Geoff was left to lead the AWD on his own. Then it was decided that two officers were required and Major Carrick seized the opportunity to substitute himself for my role in the AWD. So far as I was able to make out, someone somewhere discovered what was going on, and insisted that I was recalled to 1st Airborne. Not difficult from an administrative point of view, as at that time the SAS were under the command of the Airborne army. My special forces career was very short-lived and could be measured in hours. The OC had no option in the matter and I arrived at Blakewell Farm embarkation camp, even more frustrated than Jack, thinking that this was just another abortive operation which looked like ruining any hope I had of seeing action in Europe.

A similar mystery surrounds our CREME Lieutenant-Colonel Kinvig, who was supposed to be in the airborne assault. He was also substituted, by his adjutant Captain F W Ewens. Both substitutes finished up as wounded prisoners of war, so obviously, Lady Luck did not approve of alterations to the original plan.

Our REME Workshops had an allocation of four Horsa gliders for the Arnhem invasion, two carrying a jeep and trailer each and

1st Airborne Division October 1945 REME

the others, troops with their motorcycles, hand trailers and folding bikes etc. After my sudden return from the SAS it was too late for me to switch to my own Motor Transport staff and equipment, so for convenience, I simply took the OC's place in the glider carrying the wireless repair trailer and jeep. Apart from the two glider pilots, the only other troops on board were Craftsman Tracy-Bower and Driver Gould (who I thought was from our unit, but who later appeared on casualty lists as a CREME driver).

Our AWD was not the sole representative of REME at Arnhem. There must have been a real last minute reshuffle because, apart from myself, many others from the workshops were drafted to various units. This is best illustrated by the summary of casualties prepared by DDME shortly after the battle (*see p. 32*). According to this, 75 REME men fought at Arnhem, 35 with the AWD, 27 already on permanent attachment to various fighting units and 13 men from Divisional Workshops supplemented these at the last minute. The unlucky thirteen took the heaviest casualties: two men killed in action, seven posted as missing, and three out the four who escaped back across the river,

18

and probably did so because they had been re-united with the AWD.

The 1st Airborne Division never recovered from its heavy losses at Arnhem. Plans were drawn up to use the still under-strength Division to capture Norway by a parachute drop, but the Germans surrendered before this took place. What could have been another costly battle finished up as a convalescing occupation force, the planes flying in to unopposed landings.

The workshops in Norway were sited close to Oslo in what had been a Luftwaffe barracks, and life appears to have been quite relaxing until early June 1945, when news was received that the older members of 6th Airborne Division were to be amalgamated into 1st Division, whilst the younger men in 1st Division were to be transferred to the 6th for service in the Far East. The 220 odd people in 1st Airborne Division Workshops had been together for a long time, so this information was not received with wild enthusiasm. For compensation most of them returned to the UK for their embarkation leave carrying 'souvenirs' which had been liberated. One of them brought back a fur coat for his wife, chosen because he liked the colour! It was for a very buxom lady so his wife, who was very slim, took it to a furrier for alteration. It turned out to be a rare and very expensive model which the furrier exchanged for one to the wife's taste plus enough money to put down a house deposit. His colleagues, who had concentrated on alcoholic booty, mourned their loss.

On 9 October 1945, the Commander in Chief of the General Staff, Field Marshal Lord Brooke, wrote to General Urqhuart notifying him of the decision to disband 1st Airborne. Major Jack Carrick took the opportunity to record his unit for posterity on a photograph. Unfortunately, at this stage, it had lost most of its younger members who had been replaced with older men from 6th Airborne Division, so it is not a true representation of the unit in its 1944 heyday.

To say that it was a sad day when this fantastic division was disbanded is the biggest understatement of the century.

CHAPTER 2

The Battle of Arnhem

On the morning of 18 September 1944 we sat waiting for the jerk on the glider tow-line which would signal the start of our flight from Down Ampney to Arnhem. I looked towards the rear of the glider and remembered a narrow escape on an earlier training flight when the tow-rope parted at a critical stage during take-off. On that occasion we did not, as now, have jeep and overweight trailer on board, which in my biased eyes, given the same failure as before, would without doubt convert us into five red splotches.

To take my mind off these morbid thoughts I glanced down at my notepad to check that there was no additional information which could be entered in my War Diary at this stage of the operation:

Date	18 Sept 1944
Operation	Market Garden
Unit	Advanced Workshop Detachment 1st Airborne Div Workshop REME
Transport Mode	Horsa Glider
REME Troops	Lt H R Roberts
	Cfn Tracy-Bower
	Driver Gould
Equipment	Jeep & Wireless Repair Trailer
Take-off	....
Arrival at D.Z.	....
Flight Time	....

A warning shout from the two glider pilots that our Dakota was taking in the slack of the tow-rope just gave me sufficient time to

Wartime Europe and the location of Arnhem

glance at my watch and enter 11.00hrs against 'Take-off' before the anticipated jerk indicated that, at last, we were on our way.

The Horsa was not my favourite form of transport. It was a flimsy plywood contraption which bucked and swayed in the tug's slipstream. I much preferred parachuting, especially from Dakotas. On this occasion, however, take-off was perfect and soon we were in formation on the 'Northern' route which, unfortunately for the morale of poor swimmers like myself, involved a hundred mile sea-crossing.

There being nothing else to do at this stage, I decided that a 'cat-nap' would be the best way to ameliorate the rigours of a projected four hour flight and also to catch up with sleep lost over the last few hectic days. I was soon in the arms of Morpheus, only to be woken up as we crossed into enemy territory and anti-aircraft flak started rocking our glider.

Once awake, the call of nature to discharge some of the many cups of tea drunk before take-off reached an uncomfortable urge. The urinal facilities in a Horsa were very basic, and consisted of a rubber tube with a funnel on the end of it for the user to discharge into. I had never used one previously on training flights; nobody did if possible. There was no privacy and the occasion could be guaranteed to produce ribald and pornographic comment from bored onlookers.

I clasped the urinal funnel with my left hand whilst my right hand tried to take aim. That was when the trouble started: with both hands occupied and the glider bucking like a wild west bronco, the only way I could keep my balance was to spread my legs away from the side of the glider whilst resting my head on it. This three-point suspension gave sufficient support to enable the demands of nature to be met, but I was glad that my audience was numerically limited because the necessary stance would have added fuel to the anonymous *sotto voce* comments which were always heard on such occasions.

I had just reached that blissful stage, which can only be achieved after emptying a full bladder, when the glider bucked even more violently than usual and the Dutch landscape suddenly appeared in a draughty hole between my legs. I hastily returned my private member back into the trousers – it is surprising what false confidence you have in his safety once he is buttoned up again – and spent the remainder of the journey trying to calculate the shrapnel projectory from the entrance and exit holes in relation to my earlier position. It had been too close for comfort, but we were probably luckier than most of the other gliders because there were only a few other shrapnel holes; both the jeep and trailer appeared to be undamaged.

I was too wide awake now to return to my slumbers, so we all settled down for a chat on the irrelevant subjects which troops always seem to choose in moments of stress. Both my men, Craftsman Tracy-Bower and Driver Gould, were calm and collected as the conversation turned to a review of the forthcoming unloading drill and we stripped the small packs off our webbing to give us more freedom for the strenuous work ahead. Nobody anticipated any trouble during the actual landing, as our landing zones (LZs) were being defended by approximately half of the troops who had landed the previous day.

At 15.05hrs the LZ appeared in view in front of us, and suddenly, instead of the violent noisy movement of a towed glider, all was quiet and peaceful; we had cast-off. I peered over the shoulders of the pilots; it was quite a spectacle: gliders and parachutes covering the ground like daisies in a meadow.

The first pilot maintained a steady glide so I knew that he was selecting a landing place before committing us to that terrifying nose-dive which always made me wish for stronger anchor points on the jeep. The second pilot shouted and pointed to a promising landing strip; down went the nose. I had left it too late to get back to my seat so I wedged myself behind the two pilots. However, almost simultaneously, a glider in front of us disintegrated in mid-air and another one slipped down sideways, out of control.

Our pilot banked away from this obvious 'killing-zone' and, with only seconds left to choose an alternative spot, he followed another group of gliders going in a different direction. It had been a brilliant piece of aeronautical improvisation and I

Dropping Zones near Wolfheze station

thanked my lucky stars for the quality of our two glider pilots.

As soon as we landed I jumped out, whilst the glider was still rolling, followed by Driver Gould and Craftsman Tracy-Bower. There was a burst of fire from a spandau which fatally wounded Gould and hit me in the spine; fortunately, it missed Tracy-Bower who dived for shelter behind the wheels of the glider.

I was lucky, as every doctor has since told me. Although the bullet was fired from point-blank range, I was probably flexing in mid-air when it hit me and it went through the rubber folds of the gas mask which we carried across the small of our backs. Later, it was found that the bullet had a pronounced bend on the tip, so that it must have hit something hard *en route* into my body. Whatever it was saved my life because, after chipping my spine between the fifth and sixth vertebra without breaking the spinal chord, it somersaulted through the back muscles, stopping just short of a vital organ.

Paralysed from the waist downwards, I had no chance of escape and refused Tracy-Bower's shouted offer of help. According to him, both pilots had also been hit and appeared to be dead. I told him to forget us and try to make his own way back to our lines. As he commenced his run, our defence perimeter troops who, of necessity, had stopped firing when we flew across their field of fire, opened up with everything including smoke. His luck held and he made it to the cover of the adjacent trees. Not only was he the only survivor to escape from four Horsas which landed virtually inside the German lines, he also escaped injury in the ensuing battle around the Hartenstein hotel in Oosterbeek, before safely crossing the river with the remnants of the AWD nine days later.

I tried to drag myself over to my driver Gould to give him morphia, which all officers carried, but the loss of all movement below the waist, coupled with the drag on my webbing, made progress painfully slow. Bullets were buzzing all over the place and suddenly I heard several hit the bodies all round me and there were no further sounds of life.

In working my way over to my driver, I had entered what looked like a shallow gully which ran in the direction of some trees where I could discern some movement. It was too far to shout for help above the noise so it would be necessary to drag myself most of the way, a distance which appeared beyond my residual strength. The quandary was settled when a figure moved into clearer view: he was a German.

After laboriously turning around to go the other way I discovered that the gully faded out in the opposite direction, which I assumed would lead to our own lines, so escape that way was impossible.

In situations like this your brain either freezes or accelerates; mine went into overdrive. There was no pain at this stage, only the dreadful paralysis below the waist. The exertions over the last few minutes had effectively demonstrated what limited movements I was capable of, and the thought of spending the rest of my life in a wheelchair presented a quality of life which I could not face up to.

Once again my useless body had to be dragged around to its previous position – a lot easier this time because I had the sense to slip out of my webbing. I had my Lee-Enfield rifle Mk4, with which I had a love affair that started a long time ago when I joined the Local Defence Volunteers (LDV) in April 1940. Being the only teenager in a platoon of seasoned World War I veterans ensured a training second-to-none. Brought up on that rifle, it was always my preferred weapon. A barn door was safe from my marksmanship with our issue 9mm Browning pistols at twenty yards and I disliked the Sten gun whose unnecessary crudeness of manufacture offended my engineering susceptibilities.

The thought of ending it all with a Mills grenade received a brief consideration, until I accepted the possibility of getting a German in my sights; a vague hope but more in keeping with my Scorpio character than suicide.

The physical effort involved in recent movements had left me shattered, so, whilst the strength drained back, I emptied all the spare cartridge clips out of the pouch and laid them out in a neat row. Not that I anticipated using them all, but, having been trained in the LDV to be miserly in the use of ammunition, it was nice to feel that I could blaze away with reckless abandon. This was followed by a check on the safety catch and the half-opening of the bolt, to ensure that there was a round in the breech. I lay resting in a reclining position to ease my aching arms and shoulders, studying the beautiful woodgrain on the rifle butt and breathing in the faint smell of oil, as if it was an aphrodisiac.

Assuming the target was still there, and, given the element of surprise, it should be possible with my fast bolt action to get the best part of a magazine off before anyone located the source of fire. After that I mused, with my stomach and other vulnerable organs being partially protected in the gully, with a bit of luck I would never feel the head or heart shot which could kill me. Then, as if on cue, the wail of the bagpipes came over loud and clear. This was an omen which could not be ignored and the body reacted simultaneously with the brain as I levered up into a firing position.

It was like a dream come true. At such close range it was impossible to miss and one round was all that was required. I finished off the magazine into the undergrowth where the German fell, and, as the last cartridge was being ejected, another German ran across my field of fire. Too late! I hit the dirt cursing my luck. Bullets were humming over my head as I hugged the ground and reviewed the situation. There was no doubt that I was lucky to escape. The whole episode had been, in my own assessment, rather amateurish; admittedly, I had evened-up the score a little, but to blaze away like that was pathetic. I made a cold clinical decision since the nature of my wound had eradicated any emotion of fear or responsibility.

The object of the exercise was to take as many of the enemy with me as possible, at the same time trying to ensure maximum protection from a stomach wound. Once again, I recalled all the training given to me by my World War I sniper mentor. It was difficult to repress thoughts of home and family – very difficult – but it was necessary. There was no place for love, hope or beauty in my life, just bloody revenge.

The firing above my head was now more intermittent, but there was still no doubt that I was in the middle of a very unhealthy no-mans-land. Suddenly it dawned on me that the bullets were passing over me at approximately right-angles to my prone position, and it took some little time to work it all out. The Germans who were firing at me and our perimeter troops, were over my right shoulder, so I could not return their fire without leaving the security of my makeshift trench. On the other hand, the sitting targets I was firing at never did find out where the bullets were coming from. I was enjoying a concealed tangential view of their positions, but of course, was exposing myself sideways to their colleagues every time I opened fire.

Snug in the security of my gully, I made preparations for a change in role from rapid fire to sniper. Off came my red beret and brass cap badge: they made too good a target and would be much better employed as a pillow. I do not think that the effort to camouflage my face would have been very effective because spittle was in short supply and the earth difficult to get at.

In an effort to avoid detection I spread my elbows wide, just sufficient to aim the rifle and reload at ground level. Unfortunately, after the initial glut, targets were few and far between, and the few that appeared were half concealed. At that short range, under normal firing conditions, this would not have been much of a problem, but it was necessary to use snap shots because I only had two or three seconds before my appearance attracted enemy fire from my right flank.

How long this role lasted is difficult to estimate because I was physically exhausted, my arms and shoulders felt as though they were ready to drop off; the heat from our burning glider, coupled with the loss of blood, was just sufficient to make me drowsy, so I spent longer and longer in resting mode. The end came quite suddenly; a routine sighting revealed three clear targets setting up a machine-gun. I could not believe my luck, and again, I forgot all basic self-preservation – especially the old soldier's habit of never letting three men light their cigarettes off one match. (This is based on the supposition that a sniper sees the first man, takes aim at the second man, and shoots the third man).

All fatigue vanished as the adrenalin rushed through my veins. This time I was up on near vertical elbows to maximise visibility, and my marksmanship finally paid credit to those old sweats who had so patiently moulded the rifle into an integral part of my body. The first was easy. Bullets were whizzing round me as I took the second, but what happened to the third will forever remain a mystery. I can vaguely recall a blow to my head and then everything blacked out. Some time later I recovered consciousness thinking that if this was heaven, something was wrong with our earthly preconceptions. The whole of one side of my face ached, there was blood all over the place and then it dawned on me that I was still on the Landing Zone.

A finger exploration of my head to trace the new wound revealed nothing; all it did was to transfer some loose hairs into my mouth. The subsequent retching did nothing to improve morale. Finally, in desperation, I eased a stainless steel mirror out of my breast pocket to trace where the blood was coming from. The mystery was not cleared up immediately, because the source of the blood was my nose and mouth, but where was the bullet hole? I solved the mystery, more by accident than design, as I pushed the rifle away from me to stop the blood from dripping on to it. A bullet had smashed right into the rifle bolt area rendering it completely inoperative; presumably, the force of this impact had damaged my face.

My private war was over. A pistol was useless in my immobilised situation, so I reached for my webbing to take out a Mill's grenade, and had just settled down again when there was another burst of firing. This time I had the dubious pleasure of hearing, as well as feeling, the bullet which went straight through my right shoulder muscles and missed my spine by about an inch.

There was no way I could physically check the flow of blood from three inaccessible areas of my body. I was now immobilised from a military point of view, except for the grenade which was still firmly in my grip. There was nothing else to do except leave it to fate and hope that our side won the battle still raging above my head. We did win this particular skirmish and, later on, one of our stretcher parties collected me and pronounced the other three men dead.

I was taken by the stretcher party to their first-aid post at Wolfheze. There they discovered seventeen bullet holes in my smock, only three of these involved me. Obviously, the fact that I had removed my webbing in the sheltering gulley allowed the smock to balloon up and the Germans aimed too high. After my wounds were dressed I was moved to the Hotel Vreewijk at

Hotel Vreewijk at Oosterbeek crossroads

Oosterbeek crossroads which was occupied by our troops as a casualty clearing station. There followed a very noisy and painful nine days. The initial absence of any pain whatsoever had been replaced by an excruciating pain in my stomach. It was here that many casualties of the battle were treated by RAMC personnel until 23 September when the Germans came and declared that we were prisoners of war. My ultimate destination was Oflag IX A/Z near Rotenberg in Germany.

In all, seventy-five REME personnel went into Arnhem by air, including five officers and seventy other ranks. During the nine days of the battle there were 60 per cent casualties as summarised in the following table:

REME Casualties at Arnhem

	Officers	*Other Ranks*	*Totals*
Into Action	5	70	75
Returned to UK (including wounded)	2	28	30
Killed	–	8	8
Wounded & POW	2	10	12
Missing	1	24	25

45 Casualties (Killed + Wounded & POW + Missing)

The Advanced Workshop Detachment, who led the REME Workshops into action, consisted of two officers, Lieutenant G Manning and myself, together with thirty-three other ranks. We were dropped at Arnhem in four Horsa gliders whose loads were made up as follows:

Glider 1 (Lieutenant Manning)	Jeep and Trailer
Glider 2 (Lieutenant Roberts)	Jeep and Trailer
Glider 3 (ASM Reeds)	350 Matchless motor-cycles,
Glider 4 (AQMS Turner)	handcarts and folding bicycles

The two gliders, with ASM Reeds and AQMS Turner in charge, carried most of the AWD other ranks.

The fate of my glider and its REME personnel has been related in this chapter. All four gliders were delayed on take-off owing to inclement weather. Lieutenant Manning's glider landed at 15.10hrs and the unloading was completed in fifteen minutes without casualties. ASM Reeds' glider landed at about the same time and unloading was completed in ten minutes, under desultory sniping. AQMS Turner's glider also landed without any opposition and their unloading was carried out in fifteen minutes. The three surviving glider groups met at Wolfheze Station around 17.10hrs, before moving off to their designated DMA[1] where they dug in.

The mixed fortunes of other REME personnel at Arnhem has been difficult to trace in detail, but the following account begins with the involvement of the Commander of the REME personnel (CREME) in the 1st Airborne Division.

Our CREME, Lieutenant Colonel Kinvig, was not in the best of health prior to Arnhem, and, in point of fact, he had to retire from the army because of ill-health, shortly afterwards. Consequently, the OC of the Workshops was always having to stand-in for him, which left Division Workshops a bit short on the ground. In any event, it is most unlikely to have affected REME efficiency at Arnhem or any other foreseeable action.

Presumably because of ill-health, our CREME did not fly in with other Corps Commanders, instead his Adjutant Captain Ewens took over command. His glider took off from Fairford, a few miles from Down Ampney, which hosted our Advanced Workshop Detachment. For some unknown reason, Captain Ewens only had his Sergeant-clerk with him; perhaps they were sharing a glider with other Divisional staff. Craftsman Greaves, his batman/driver travelled in an AWD glider and finally joined-up with them at 18.00hrs. The only other member of CREME's party was Driver Gould who travelled in my glider and was killed on landing.

1   Divisional Maintenance Area

Arnhem and surrounding area

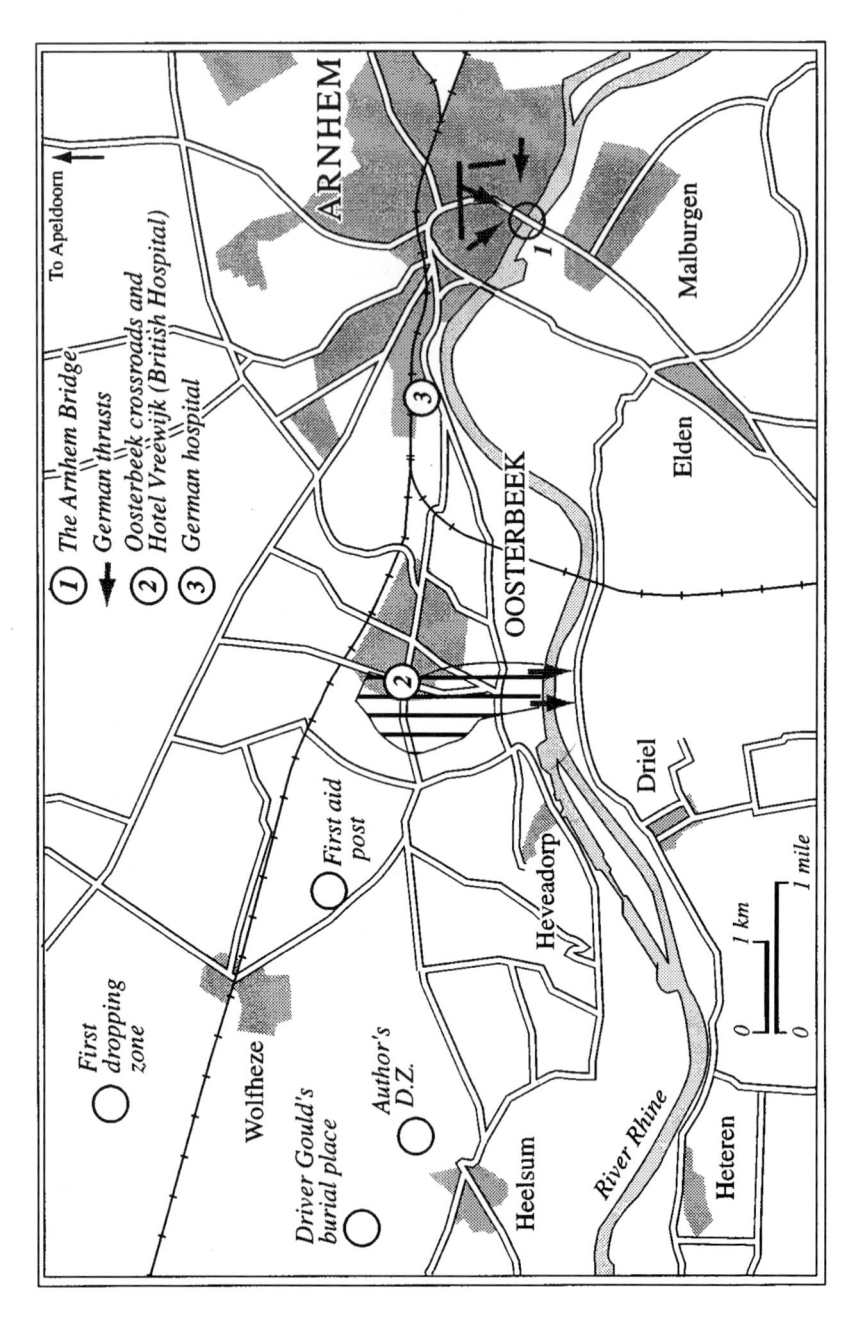

CREME's glider had a relatively uneventful flight, except for some minor flak over the Dutch coast. It made a perfect landing in a ploughed field. The War Diary, unfortunately, does not define the LZ, but they came under machine gunfire on landing at 15.25hrs, much later than my glider. The tail was detached and unloading was completed in fifteen minutes. They made a rendezvous at Wolfheze railway crossing at 16.00hrs, arriving at the Divisional HQ twenty-five minutes later. After a short pause they moved with Divisional HQ to the Hartenstein Hotel in Oosterbeek and dug-in, having acquired their two glider pilots for back-up. As stated earlier, the AWD reported their arrival and location at 18.30hrs.

Early next morning, 19 September, they moved HQ CREME into a house approximately 500 yards from Divisional HQ. There they requisitioned five vehicles from an adjacent garage and sent them to the AWD to make them mobile. Already, at this early stage, they were under continuous sniper fire, together with slight mortar fire. Verbal orders were received to move their CREME HQ back to Divisional HQ, as a strong enemy attack was developing in their sector. On their return to Divisional HQ, they received news of their driver's death (Gould) in the AWD glider.

On the following day, 21 September, HQ CREME was re-established at the previous location, the German attack having been beaten off. In retaliation, the enemy cut off the water supply. Captain Ewens visited the AWD to pick up a message but, on his way to Divisional HQ, he had an argument with a mortar bomb. A severe wound in the thigh necessitated hospital treatment, which meant that Lieutenant Manning had to fill his vacancy. With only two officers left out of four, Geoff Manning ordered the remainder of CREME HQ staff to return to Divisional HQ location. Captain R Hayward, who was EME to the Royal Artillery in the 1st Airborne, was on the battlefield but must have been sited some distance away from Divisional HQ because, as the senior officer, he should have taken over CREME's job when Ewens was wounded.

By now, the German bombardment was incessant and early next

The Hartenstein Hotel, Oosterbeek

Typical damage caused at the Battle of Arnhem in the Oosterbeek area

day, 22 September, the small group suffered its next casualty when one of the glider pilots was wounded by shell fire and taken to hospital. At this stage all food was exhausted and even the water from an adjacent well had dried up. On 23 September, their jeep finally succumbed to the incessant mortar and shell fire, and the remaining glider pilot was recalled by his CO as the situation got more and more desperate.

24 September was a veritable nightmare, with constant enemy thrusts which had to be repelled; there was no further space for the perimeter defences to contract to – as it was they were nearly fighting back-to-back. Finally, on 25 September orders were

received to withdraw all troops to the north bank of the Rhine, and to try and cross the river into the small sector on the south bank held by our relieving forces.

The REME contingent was divided into two groups, one under the command of Lieutenant Manning and the other under Lieutenant Brodie's command. The two surviving members from the CREME establishment were in Lieutenant Manning's party. They left the HQ location around 21.04hrs, following tapes laid out as guides, each man holding on to the tail of the smock of the man in front. On route they encountered heavy machine gun fire and had to divert into woods, skirting around enemy patrols, finally reaching the north bank about 00.30hrs on 26 September: three hours to cover a distance under one mile. The promised evacuation boats were nowhere to be seen, but a search produced various small craft, which enabled some survivors to reach the other bank in scattered batches between 02.45 and 04.30hrs.

The REME party reached Nijmegen at 16.00hrs on 27 September and joined Major Carrick's seaborne party at 06.30hrs on 28 September, before leaving within a few hours for Louvain; twenty of them caught a plane for the UK on the following day. The remaining five other ranks had to wait until 30 September before they emplaned for the UK.

CHAPTER 3

Prisoner of War

This chapter starts in an Army Casualty Clearing Station at Oosterbeek in Holland, when the Germans evacuated us from the battle of Arnhem on Monday, 25 September 1944 and is based on a war diary which I maintained until final repatriation on Wednesday, 18 April 1945.

The first part was written on scraps of paper and was rewritten in a 'Wartime Log for British Prisoners' donated by the YMCA and issued to us when we arrived at our Oflag. Thereafter it was maintained on a daily basis.

Because it could be seized and scrutinised by the Germans, of necessity anything of a secret nature could not be written in one's script. Whilst lying in the Oflag hospital there was plenty of time to develop a complicated secret code to identify items which I wanted to be personal. In the early part of the diary it will be noted from a specimen page, there was unnecessary use of many capital letters and the odd cryptic word out of context. Unfortunately, after forty-five years, when I ultimately started to type it all out, I could not recall the vaguest idea of how the code operated. Originally, every little detail was faithfully transcribed in the hope the penny would drop. However, the code remained as elusive as ever and finally, the draft was adjusted to eliminate abbreviations and army vernacular to make it more understandable to the general reader. It is emphasized that this, in no way has altered the original content of the diary.

At a later stage in the diary the code was abandoned – it got too complicated to operate as I got more and more involved in

2

Field Ambulance – Arnhem

Gallantry of Cpl – s/self removal by goons
mattresses on floor – glass danger – morphia to ease stomach pain – sicken
by self-prop. shot roof off – continuous mortar fire – bombs on verandah –
captured by goons – by wounded tonight & a then removed – rainwater
episode.

Subjects discussed by men – excellent morale + spirits – beer, places visit
women, judgement on latter re Yanks, Eyes, & Goons. No war

Cpl + pte re-setting dislocated shoulders etc.

No violence offered by goons after capturing us. S.S. s/major spoke
disparagingly of standard of the mixed tpsunder his command.
These SS certainly are tough birds. Same as us, merciless in battle
but good captors afterwards.

Tremendous nervestrain from continuous murderous mortar fire, but
think I could have held out much longer. Combined with dirt + darkness
situation was pretty grim.

Ack/Ack pretty terrific on both sides. Gallantry of RAF re-supply.
Polish paras get hell knocked out of them. Tiffys busy with their rockets
I wish they'd bash the blasted S.P. outside.

Glider pilots seem to have had the shit knocked out of them
Bits of mortar bombs flying all over the place.

Transference of some wounded to the hospital

Rations very short, even water, not that it worried me much, but oh boy did I
enjoy that tea.

Oakehill Farm
Down Ampney
TO.   11·0
Arr   3·5
       4 tas

Specimen pages from author's diary. See overleaf for transcription

40

...ransferred to a converted hospital at Apeldoorn
...German ambulances on Monday 25th Sept 1944.
...hundreds of refugees on the road
...rst meal consisted of 1/5 loaf of bread and butter
...fect of light caused considerable increase in general
...ll-being and appetite.
...ood very short, potato ration increased.
...irst shave since landing on the Tuesday.
...ot out of bed for the first time on Monday,
...nd Oct exactly a fortnight after being wounded.
...ve myself a bath in a bowl, needed it badly.
...ceived first news of unit. Harvey killed, shrapnel
...rough Reed, Green, Gray, Lee, Jordan, L/Cpl Graham,
...owerson wounded, S/Sgt (Ind) captured. Capt Evens
... hospital with broken leg.
...umours about 2nd Army but no real gen.
...ounds continue to heal up marvelously
...irit and morale of men very high.
...ransferred to hospital officers ward.

NOTES

This copy of two pages from Captain Roberts' War Diary has been retouched for reproduction. It is still difficult to read by virtue of the very small handwriting and for this reason the following transcript is given of page 2. The contents of the two pages shown relate to the author being taken prisoner whilst lying wounded in the First Aid Post at the Hotel Vreewijk at the Oosterbeek crossroads on Tuesday, 19 September 1944 and the days following leading to transfer to the German (Elizabeth) controlled Hospital and subsequent move to Apeldoorn (Sept 25).

Page 2 of War Diary Transcript

Field Ambulance – Arnhem

Gallantry of Corporal – S/Sgt removal by Goons

Mattresses on floor – glass danger – morphia to ease stomach pain-sickness

G-Self-prop. shot roof off – continuous mortar fire – bombs on veranda – capture by goons – G wounded tonight and then removed – rainwater episode.

Subjects discussed by men – excellent morale & spirits – beer, places visited, women, judgement on latter re Yanks, Eyes & Goones. No war. Cpl & pts resettling dislocated shoulders, etc.

No violence offered by Goons after capturing us. SS S/Major spoke disparagingly of standard of the mixed tps under his command.

These SS certainly are tough birds. Same as us, merciless in battle but good captors afterwards.

Tremendous nerve strain from continuous mortar fire, but I think that I could have held out much longer. Combined with dirt and darkness situation was pretty grim.

Ack/Ack pretty terrific on both sides. Gallantry of RAF re-supply bags. Polish paras got hell knocked out of them. Tiffy's busy with their rockets.

I wish they'd bash the blasted S.P. outside.

Glider pilots seem to have had the shit knocked out of them.

Bits of mortar bombs flying all over the place.

Transference of some wounded to the hospital (Elizabeth Hospital).

Rations very short, even water, not that it worried me much, but Oh! boy did I enjoy the tea.

Blakehill Farm	
Down Ampney	This obviously refers to the take-off and arrival of Captain Roberts' flight from Blakehill Farm at Down Ampney to the Arnhem Dropping Zone. (Ed).
TO 11.0	
Arr 3.5	
4 Hrs	

various activities. Instead, security items were entered in a more open manner using innocuous wording. These sections can still be identified together with the appropriate dates.

Memory is a funny thing. Over the intermediate years I have been able to recall vividly certain episodes in my POW life, but others only came back to me during the transcript into type. Other episodes in the diary still remain a complete blank in my memory.

Not many POWs kept a complete diary because the monotony of prison life tended to sap away initiative. Even in my own case, the unfinished letter to my fiancée and the monotony of the central entries illustrate apathy. I tried to maintain it for two principal reasons, first to act as a reminder when I got back to the UK. A good enough reason, but one which has taken half-a-century to get around to. Probably the real reason was the second one and that was the optimistic hope that if ever I was killed, someone or other would send it back to my next of kin so that they would have some idea of what had happened to me.

Apart from the diary element, the book was also used to record miscellaneous statistical data – none of which I have ever got round to reading since I wrote it.

This first section of my POW life is written in a conventional book style for easy assimilation.

Prisoner of war life started for me on 23 September 1944, lying seriously wounded and starkers, except for my socks, under one blanket – on the floor in the semi-darkness of a Regimental First Aid Post – under artillery bombardment, at the Hotel Vreewijk on the Oosterbeek crossroads near Arnhem.

Some days earlier all my clothes had been removed by the simple process of slitting them up the back, but fortunately, the remnants of the battledress blouse and trousers had been stuffed into my pillowcase so I retained all the possessions in those pockets. All the other bloodstained clothing, camouflage smock, shirt, vest and pants, etc had been thrown away, together with my boots as the left one had its heel shot off. By a stroke of real good fortune I still possessed my red beret without which any Airborne soldier really does feel naked.

Following a burst of activity and shouting outside the building, everything went quiet, then the door opened and a very large SS Sergeant-major walked in. With a nonchalant wave of his revolver he said in immaculate English: 'Gentlemen, you are now my prisoners'. No one spoke as he slowly walked the length of the crowded room before turning quickly on his heels to march briskly out of the door, which he did not close behind him. He was very large and quite ugly, which earned him the immediate nickname of Boris Karloff.

Shortly afterwards British and German medical orderlies started carrying out wounded officers to the Elizabeth Hospital. They missed me because, at that stage, even the British did not know my rank, as all my clothing had been removed at Wolfheze when they applied the original wound dressings and evacuated me to Oosterbeek.

I kept my rank secret, as there was always the possibility that the other ranks could be liberated if 2nd Army suddenly broke through, whereas it was obvious that officers were being transferred as far away as possible from any relief column.

Up to this point the medics had sedated me with morphine to ease the violent abdominal pain resulting from the spinal wound, but the medics had just informed me that they dare not give me any more in case I became addicted. In point of fact they had run out of supplies, but that explanation was quite acceptable to a generation brainwashed into the potential evils of drug addiction.

The doctors and senior NCOs were the next to disappear and we were left in the hands of a corporal and a few medical orderlies. There was also a young Dutch girl who had helped to carry my stretcher when we were transferred to the hospital under heavy machine-gun fire, who had stayed to help out with the nursing. Perhaps she had a parochial interest in me because every time the sounds of battle got particularly vicious she used to crouch at my side and hold my hand.

Shortly after we had been captured, when the building was rocking under heavy bombardment, some German soldiers positioned on our top floor tumbled down the stairs and, whilst hurrying to the door at the other end of the room, one of them tripped over my feet. I did not feel anything because of the paralysis, but the little Dutch girl shouted after the soldier, presumably in German. He said something in reply, which was obviously of a threatening nature, so I thought I had better intervene. Of course, not knowing much German, my response had to be in English, but by the time I had finished, no one in the room was under any misapprehension regarding my rank, including the German soldier. I am not sure if it was a near miss on the balcony outside, or my vernacular which speeded his departure.

Some time afterwards 'Boris Karloff' reappeared on the scene and started to walk slowly down the room, carefully looking at each man in turn. Realising that I had been rumbled I put on my 'officer's voice' and called him over. He did not waste any time in demanding my rank, name and number, which I just as promptly gave him. It was rather unbelievable; he clicked his heels together and I would swear that he was just about to stand to attention when he remembered that he was our captor. Then he wanted to know why I had not been evacuated with the other officers, at which stage the RAMC corporal intervened to say that up to then I had been under heavy sedation and even they did not know my rank. Anyway, the very nature of my wounds and the associated paralysis meant that I could only be moved under the supervision of a doctor. He seemed quite happy with this explanation, so I moved on to the attack. First of all I flattered him by saying what a reputation the fighting SS enjoyed with the Airborne – no lie this, because it was quite true – and I knew, therefore, that the troops who scuttled down from their posts on the roof every time things got a bit sticky did not belong to that élite force. However, they were under his command so could he please order them not to injure the wounded further in their panic rush to safety, especially as it involved the loss of face of fighting men in front of a girl who stayed at her post.

I thought that I had gone a bit too far, but fortunately his anger was not directed at me. I would have loved a translation of what he said to his men later on – whatever it was, it was more than effective.

Boris Karloff was definitely not the type of man anyone would want to meet on a dark night but he and I hit it off together. I know that many of his compatriots earned an evil reputation, but he never put a finger wrong as far as I was concerned. He was the first of many Germans to give me the line 'This is stupid, you and I should not be fighting each other: we should join forces to fight the Russian Bear'. At that time this sounded nonsense so I diplomatically kept quiet and nodded my head.

He spoke disparagingly about the mixed bunch of troops under his command. Apparently, his own unit had been virtually wiped out in the Falaise Gap and the remaining survivors had split up to command odds and sods from other retreating units. He was far from happy in this new role. We had been suffering from thirst because the water supplies had been cut off. He rectified this by making his men collect water from rain butts, a rather hazardous job as they came under fire from their own troops.

After our capture no further British casualties were brought in, but the evacuation of the officers and dead bodies created space, which was then filled with German casualties: Boris Karloff visited us, presumably to check that we were not fighting each other. When he found one of our lads lighting a cigarette for a German who had lost an arm, he walked round distributing cigarettes to all and sundry, like a benevolent Father Christmas. He was quite a character. We never saw him again after the cigarette distribution, which left us wondering if he had been killed or simply moved forward as the German net closed around the Hartenstein defence perimeter.

It was amazing how wounded men maintained their spirits and morale. The subjects they discussed whilst lying in agony in filth and dirt, with the whole building shaking under incessant bombardment and death around the corner, would defy any modern welfare state psychologist. Food was a popular subject; each man would outline his favourite meal, the subsequent conversation regarding the respective merits between, for example roast, boiled or chipped potatoes, sometimes got a little intense. The ladies, as one might expect, were well in the forefront of the discussions, especially from the old sweats who took the opportunity to finish off the sexual education of their younger brethren, with all supporting details. English girls did not come out very high in the international ratings but, no doubt this was strongly influenced by recent shortages due to the large number of Americans who had invaded the happy hunting grounds.

One crippled para had received a 'Dear John' letter just prior to take-off and this probably had a stronger influence on the voting than the American competition. The unanimous decision of the impromptu kangaroo court was that only Airborne could be trusted.

Just prior to capture, one man had been brought in with a serious bullet wound through the chest, and another which had shot away one of his testicles. It was routine to enquire what injuries new patients had received, and I can vividly recall the horrified whispering when details of his lower injury were circulated. It was the general consensus of opinion that it would be more merciful if he died from the chest wound; a view echoed by the casualty himself when he recovered consciousness. The corporal's opinion that this would not affect his future sexual activity was greeted with sheer disbelief, together with rude remarks on his professional competence. Even the subsequent confirmation by the staff-sergeant was not entirely convincing to the despondent officer and his equally morbid audience. It was not until a pre-war sweat recalled a comparable accident some years ago in India, that partial relief swept through the ward.

The respective qualities and tastes of beer and cigarettes was yet another constant topic of conversation. This was mostly above my head because I did not smoke and, to me, beer was just beer! However, after listening to the experts contrasting Newcastle ale against Liverpool beer, I came to the conclusion that I must have a deficiency in my taste buds.

Writing this out in full, after nearly half-a-century, makes me wonder how we coped. Seriously wounded and dying men, lying shoulder to shoulder on the floor of a building, slowly disintegrating under incessant bombardment; windows shattering and plaster falling on your head as shrapnel and bullets buried themselves in the walls just above your heads; minimum food and water, with the spectre of death at everyone's shoulder. Indeed, in some of our makeshift hospitals surgeons and patients were killed at the operating table, whilst other wounded men were crushed to death when the walls fell in. We were lucky; our casualties were relatively light, even though we were in the centre of the battle.

Soon after Boris Karloff disappeared, fresh German faces appeared on the scene and removed their own wounded. Then, on Monday 25 September, we were all evacuated in a miscellaneous collection of transports to an army barracks at Apeldoorn which had been converted into a temporary hospital to get the wounded fit enough to be moved further back into Germany.

I found the effect of daylight after a long period in semi-darkness most stimulating, which partially offset the disappointment of being moved further away from our own forces. Of course, at this stage we were all completely unaware of how parlous 1st Airborne's situation had become; the eventuality of our troops retreating back across the Rhine never entered our heads.

The journey to Apeldoorn did not take long, even though the roads were crowded with pathetic columns of refugees, pushing prams and handcarts stacked high with all their remaining worldly possessions. Our destination in Apeldoorn was a brick-built barracks, but it was grossly overcrowded and conditions were very mixed. I was lucky because I got a bunk; others had to sleep on the floor, but we were all feeling the cold, perhaps because we had lost the actual body warmth of our previous tight confinement.

In retrospect, the Germans had obviously done their best at very short notice because, on the very same night that our division retreated across the river, they had already despatched five hundred wounded airborne troops into Germany and evacuated another nine hundred seriously wounded to Apeldoorn.

By now, the effects of the morphine had worn off; I had terrific pain in my abdomen, even though all body movement below my spinal wound had disappeared. A combination of shock reaction, no food and little sleep for eight days, dehydration and inadequate bedding, left me very cold. But on the brighter side, the shelling was only a distant rumble, daylight was streaming through the windows and a hot drink tasted like nectar: like a wounded animal I curled up and went to sleep. As I drifted off I remember hoping that our tanks would not make too much noise when they rescued us!

I woke up shivering the following morning to find myself lying on my front, starkers as usual, and the movements on my back and the odd spoken word told me that my wounds were being re-dressed. Incidentally, to dispel any romantic Florence Nightingale illusions, this process consisted of removing the old field-dressing, swabbing off any remnants of clothing, or equipment which the bullet had injected into the wound, and which was now emerging as an evil pus, before shaking sulphanilamide powder from what looked like a glorified sugar sifter, into the bullet holes. Finally a clean dressing was applied which was simple but very effective, thanks to the people who invented antibiotics.

The medics rolled me over on to my back and it suddenly occurred to me that the German uniforms with them were different from the ones who had carried us in yesterday. They were not ordinary Wehrmacht: they had brought in crack Herman Goering troops to guard us. I was treated most properly; they were listing rank, name and number and types of wounds. I, on the other hand, was far more interested in questioning the doctors regarding the permanence or otherwise of my paralysis. They scratched my feet and saw a reaction which I personally had not felt. It was the German doctor who paused when the others went off, to offer me hope and who instructed an orderly to find me another blanket. Somehow or other, although I had not set out to deceive them, they missed my commissioned rank and I remained with my old comrades in an other ranks ward.

Life was relatively blissful after the previous week in Oosterbeek. The first meal consisted of one-fifth of a loaf of bread and butter, washed down with hot coffee made from acorns. After a week of enforced virtual starvation this disappeared into my empty stomach and was lost without trace. Of greater importance, however, was the appeal I made to any passer-by to feel my feet and the overwhelming relief which swept through me when I first felt their touch. A joy shared by all my wounded compatriots: they had already had the doctor's positive diagnosis of 'Johnny-one-ball' and were now advising him on its interest value during future sexual liaisons. His potentially lethal chest wound was fortunately showing signs of recovery.

As might be expected, morale dropped when we heard from men wounded in the break-out that the Division had retreated across the river. The bitterness which emanated from all around us about the waste of friends' lives – all for nothing – was very deep. The language was purple, in fact; if you cut out the swear words very little would be left. As for myself, all I could do was wonder why they could not throw a Bailey bridge across to the bridgehead which had been bought at so heavy a human cost. I think my lifelong cynicism regarding the limited intelligence of the 'establishment' was conceived in that hospital bunk.

The casual medic-patient attitudes which prevailed in our Oosterbeek casualty clearing station were soon forgotten as military hospital discipline was quickly implemented. Before the end of the first day all unshaven faces were targeted for action. About mid-afternoon I was presented with a basin of cold water, a small piece of soap, a safety razor and told to get a shave. Even under favourable conditions this would have been uncomfortable: it felt as though two or three hundred men had already shared the razor blade. It was absolute agony hacking away at the stubble and I just could not manage to trim my upper lip; every time I tried my eyes watered, so I decided to grow a moustache. After that first day, for some reason or other, the razor blades seemed much sharper but my moustache remained intact.

I think it must have been fairly early on in Apeldoorn that some of my own REME craftsmen found me and brought me up to date with our own casualty list. I can vaguely recall the incident, but the details are a little vague, so it was probably before I started to recover from my paralysis. After that, my whole character changed: there is an old saying that 'the sword must go through the fire before it can be tempered'. Until you have plunged to the depths of despair you never appreciate just how good the simple things in life really are. People never realise how lucky they are until they lose something and then it is often too late. I was lucky to recover my mobility, and since that time have tried to count my blessings and accept life as it unfolded.

The next few days were uneventful. Rumours were circulating about colleagues escaping over to the Dutch underground, but my physical condition left no hope in that direction. However, there were some encouraging signs of recovery, my stomach torture progressively eased away and my normal body functions became less erratic. Even the doctors' scratch tests on my feet became more distinct. I cannot claim that my morale increased pro rata because the doctors would not commit themselves as to whether or not I would regain the use of my legs.

This state of limbo lasted exactly one week in Apeldoorn, until Monday 2 October, to be exact, fifteen days after being wounded. As usual, I woke up just after dawn, and, suddenly realised that something had changed. At first I did not realise what was wrong; my eyes swept around their limited field of vision to ascertain the reason for the animal instinct which was bothering me. Nothing; the room looked normal enough – some of my comrades seemed half-awake, others were snoring peacefully, interrupted by the odd groan as they rolled over on their wounds in their sleep. Then, panic swept over me, sheer unadulterated panic, as I suddenly realised that I could feel my right leg. The left one also felt semi-operational, but the right one felt more or less normal.

It dawned on me that the bullet in my spine must have somehow moved away from the nerve it had been pressing on, but if it could move one way, might it not move the other way, probably severing the nerve and paralysing me for life? I must admit that my first reaction was not overwhelming relief; it was

The author's POW Identity Card

panic on a scale which I had never experienced before. I froze, not daring to move; even my breathing was restricted to shallow breaths, whilst I worked out the next safe move.

The spell was broken when another patient called out for a bedpan, which was brought to him by an orderly. At that time there was a phrase in common use when things got a bit sticky: 'come on lads – shit or bust'. His request, in basic terms, triggered a clarion call in my head and cleared my thoughts. I called the orderly over after he had delivered the bedpan and asked him to support me whilst I tried to stand up. He felt he should call a doctor so I pulled rank on him. Fortunately, one of my erstwhile Oosterbeek neighbours was awake and graphically described the penalties for not obeying an officer.

The poor orderly was in a predicament; I was clinging on to the side of the bunk, physically and verbally resisting his efforts to get me back into it. The crippled cockney perched on the bedpan was urging me on and all the orderly could say was 'Oh! f*** me!' until the now enthralled audience assured him that no one fancied him but had he got a sister?

After what seemed to be an eternity the world stopped revolving in my head and I found that I could stand without any assistance from the orderly, even though most of my weight was still on my arms. Great waves of relief and emotion went through me; all morbid thoughts of the bullet moving the other way and life in a wheelchair disappeared. The orderly was sworn to secrecy regarding my rank, otherwise he could be charged with assisting the enemy by delivering me to a more closely guarded officer's ward.

For the remainder of the day, except during the routine German inspection period, I practised sitting up to eliminate the light-headedness to the encouragement of all my neighbours. By evening I was really excited at my progress and decided to go to the latrines which were, if I recall correctly, about twenty yards away. I staggered most of the way and crawled the last bit on my hands and knees. That night I slept like a babe-in-arms. When I awoke the following morning the events of the previous day came flooding back to me, so, without really thinking about it, I decided to pay another visit to the latrines to defecate.

There was no orderly in the vicinity: they were very thin on the ground at this stage, so I decided it would be safer to crawl there. After a few yards I thought that I should stand up, as it would be preferable to collapse in a relatively clean corridor rather than the unhygienic toilets. No problem really, my right leg was quite strong and, although I could not trust my left leg to move instinctively, it seemed to respond to mental directives. I walked there, had a rest whilst sitting down, and then walked back to my bunk unaided.

It seemed such a shame to lie down again; after all, I had been doing that for over a fortnight, so I decided to have a good wash. Orderlies were very scarce, I think the Germans had been shipping them back to the Fatherland, but ultimately I managed to get one to bring me a small bowl of lukewarm water, a piece of soap, and a tattered towel which itself was in great need of a wash. In spite of these limitations, I managed an all-over washdown which was a great boost to my morale. The physical progress I had made in the last twenty-four hours was fantastic, and my thoughts now turned to the possibility of escape.

A survey through the windows showed that we were now only lightly guarded as, theoretically, only the seriously wounded remained in the hospital. The Germans had moved everyone out as soon as they were strong enough; we were, after all, only a few miles from our own front line.

I was not the only wolf in sheep's clothing. There was a laddie, from the KOSBs[1] I think, who had a bullet wound in his chest and an exit wound in his side, plus a flesh wound in his thigh. In point of fact, the first bullet had not penetrated his chest, it had literally run round the rib cage before exiting. He was building up his left wound before attempting to escape.

The third member of our escape trio was a glider pilot who had been cooking some eggs and bacon which he had 'found' when

1   Kings Own Scottish Borderers

a Tiger tank pulled up underneath his bedroom vantage point. The crew got out to stretch their legs and, as they urinated, he shot them with his Sten gun. His first reaction had been to grab his half-cooked meal and then find a safer place to eat it. However, being a glider pilot, and therefore slightly mad, he decided to commandeer the tank! Unfortunately, as he climbed up its side a German patrol came round the corner and shot him. Only one bullet actually hit him, opening out his stomach like a surgeon's scalpel. As he fell he, fortunately, held his innards inside his stomach automatically. The enemy paid no further attention to him as such wounds are obvious and usually fatal. A stretcher party found him before too long and someone, he did not know who or where, stitched him up. During the initial medical inspection it had been decided, because the stitching was so crude, in all probability his innards had been stuffed back in an unhygienic condition, that his chances of survival were not very likely.

He did nothing, of course, to dispel these opinions so the three of us acted as 'unpaid shit-house wallahs' to our less fortunate friends whilst we built up our strengths ready to escape. I was the last to join the trio, who enjoyed the salubrious nicknames of 'Creeper', 'Crawler' and 'Snake', which were derived from our individual gaits.

Unfortunately, my career as a stand-in ward assistant was of short duration owing to the inconsistency of the daily German inspections. Normally they did not vary their routine but, on 4 October, for some reason, they retraced their steps. This was the third day on my feet and I was moving much more briskly. I was making a return trip from the toilets, clutching an empty urine tin in either hand, when I caught a glimpse of a German uniform just around the corner and simultaneously heard their voices. Retreat was impossible, so I adopted a haggard pose and painfully dragged myself the last few inches into their view. There was some resultant consternation and confusion, but my acting deserved an Oscar, even though I say it myself.

Having escorted me back to my bunk, everything was going well, until one of the guards tried to flatten out a bump under the mattress, before helping me back into bed. He turned the mattress back to reveal two Browning automatic pistols, some binoculars and compasses! The previous relaxed atmosphere changed to one of tense confrontation.

'*Alles kaput, alles kaput*', I kept repeating, it being one of the few German phrases I could remember. Although I had been in German hands for nearly a fortnight no one had ever searched me, and it seemed that many of the other stretcher cases had similar experiences.

During my urine collecting trips around the wards I had been given these now futile military articles for disposal. As an officer I could not refuse to take responsibility, but where could I put them? As an interim measure I stored them under my mattress, having first rendered them useless. Normally this area of the bed was covered with the turned-down blankets during the daily inspection.

My repetitive statement whilst hanging weakly on to the side of the bunk, with one foot obviously in the grave, suddenly bore fruit. The German NCO picked up one of the pistols, saw that the magazine was missing, checked that there was no bullet in the breech and then jabbered away in German. Shaking my head and drawing on my limited vocabulary, I kept telling them that I did not understand German before holding my hand for the empty pistol. After a brief pause he handed it to me, and with artificial painfully slow movements I stripped it down to show them how I had sabotaged the firing mechanism. My *pièce de résistance* in this charade was to claim indignantly that British weapons must not be allowed to fall into enemy hands!

In view of the fact that they had just acquired thousands of our weapons this brought the house down – when they finally comprehended what I was saying. They hooted with laughter. One of them took his Luger out, and from his actions, I gathered that he was trying to prove to me the superiority of his pistol to ours. I pretended to argue the case until it became obvious to them that they had won the argument. I sealed it by saying 'very good' in German, which just about exhausted my vocabulary.

By this time another guard had conducted a thorough search of my pillow case and my badges of rank had been discovered. This appeared to regularise the whole affair. From what I could gather from a later conversation with a German-speaking witness, they could not understand why an 'ordinary' soldier would want to disarm the weapons, but, as soon as they discovered that I was an officer, it was OK. Without further ado, I was loaded on a stretcher and transferred to the officers' ward in the next block. I curled up and went to sleep to keep out of any further mischief.

Next day, 5 October, we were told that we were going to be transferred to a hospital train. It was only then that I realised how inadequate was my clothing, which consisted of a red beret, a pair of socks and a battledress which was slit open up the back. Luckily, I was able to scrounge about a dozen safety-pins which held the blouse and trousers loosely together, and by cutting holes in the pillowcase, I finished up with a skin-tight vest. I then cut up part of a blanket to bind round my feet, as all spare boots had disappeared a long time ago. In retrospect, I would have been much warmer if I had used the blanket to make a shirt.

The weather was typical for October, so it will be appreciated how cold it was with the wind blowing through the pinned-up battledress. Fortunately, the journey to the railway station did not take too long and we found, to our pleasure, that it was a proper ambulance train with German orderlies and nurses. My professional instincts were aroused as, prior to entering the army one of my civilian jobs had been to convert ordinary passenger coaches into ambulance trains and, I must admit, I spent a lot of time comparing the designs of the two countries.

The train remained in the station for two whole days, but I was warm in bed, the German medics were very good, food was a little more plentiful, averaging two-and-a-half to three slices of bread for breakfast and tea. In fact, we were probably too comfortable because we tended to doze off during the daytime so that by 6.30p.m. when darkness fell, we soon had our fill of sleep and were wide awake by midnight.

Suddenly, the German medics disappeared and our own

orderlies took over again, just prior to the train setting out for Germany at 6.15p.m. on 7 October 1944. The journey was relatively uneventful. I recall that we were forbidden to look out, especially when passing through built-up areas. Together with others, I naturally broke this rule, but the sight of devastated ruins of Hanover made me lose interest in sightseeing. I thought the time opportune for taking full stock of my worldly possessions; during this I found a packet of cigarettes, presumably slipped into my pocket by a padre whilst I was unconscious.

I leaned over the side of my bunk and asked the man below if he smoked – a rather tactless query in the circumstances – as was indicated by his explicit response. It was some time ago that the last cigarette had been smoked and most people were suffering from acute withdrawal symptoms. Incidentally, the officer–other rank segregation at Apeldoorn had been ignored when the train was loaded and we were all mixed up again. Hastily, I intervened to tell him that I had an unopened packet of cigarettes and, being a non-smoker, they were of no interest to me; he could have them if the brand was to his taste. A bomb could not have caused greater excitement, the noise increased to a crescendo as each man tried to pass word down the coach. Then doubt was cast on the reality of the situation.

'Some poor bugger has gone off his rocker; no wonder; I feel like joining him'.

By now we had been joined by an orderly who was advised to sort out the poor bloke who had cracked. The insinuations about my mental state stung me to an immediate response and I told them in no uncertain terms that:

> I had an unopened packet of ten cigarettes
> I did not smoke
> I was giving them away
> Who wanted them?

It would take too long to describe in detail the resulting sequence of events so I will précis it:

Everyone must have his fair share of this heaven-sent donation.

Thank God he is a non-smoker: it would have been hell to smell someone else smoking.

Wake everyone up, even the critically wounded, so that they do not miss the opportunity of a last drag.

Instead of cutting them up, best way would be to light them one at a time and pass them round the carriage.

Problem! Some people inhale deeply, others only puff; what is the authorised duration for each person? (A most contentious point which I thought would never be resolved and I intervened to suggest that the orderly could carry it around and arbitrate on fair play. Nicotine craving had now become rather desperate, so, this was agreed although there were muted comments on the doubtful parentage of the orderly).

Heavenly bliss descended on the carriage as distribution commenced. I never had any urge to smoke and this example of nicotine addiction ensured my future abstinence. It was very difficult for me to comprehend their total addiction to tobacco, but the future value of cigarettes as a trading medium was something which stood me in good stead over the following months. Even the empty cigarette packet was gratefully received by my bunk mate, who tucked it in his pocket as though it contained a diamond instead of the lingering perfume of ciggies.

Two days after leaving Apeldoorn we arrived at Fallingbostel, which was about one mile from Stalag XIB, a huge complex of different POW camps, each holding thousands of men of different nationalities. Prior to the war it had been a concentration camp and had already claimed tens of thousands of victims of disease, neglect and typhus. Fortunately, at this stage we were blissfully unaware of its history.

It was many years after the war before I found how my deception at Apeldoorn had probably saved my life, insofar as we were the only Arnhem wounded survivors to be afforded the luxury of an ambulance train. All the others had been conveyed in dirty cattle trucks, with no food supplies and very little water. In comparison to our luxurious two-day journey, theirs was four days of hell with many men dying *en route*. With typical Teutonic mentality, the dead bodies were not unloaded when, on the second day the train was stopped to let the prisoners relieve themselves: the Stalag was expecting a given number of prisoners and it made no difference whether they were alive or dead on arrival. When they arrived at Fallingbostel everyone had to march up the Stalag hill, even if they were dying, the only exceptions being leg amputees. Once there, they were kept standing in the rain for hours awaiting interrogation. I do not think I could have survived this ordeal in my weakened semi-naked condition without boots, etc.

The lucky fairy who had adopted me on the landing zone at Arnhem was obviously still perched on my shoulder because we missed most of the extremes inflicted on our comrades. The guards must have felt that we really were critically wounded because we had been afforded the rare privilege of an ambulance train. I cannot recall how we were transported to the Stalag; it must have been by truck, otherwise I would have noted it in my diary.

The first impression was that the guards were totally different from our previous SS guards; these were just scum. It has always annoyed me over the years, when the media have grouped the fighting SS units with their political SS counterparts, who only disgraced their uniform. Everyone who encountered the fighting SS had a healthy respect for them, whereas their political colleagues, who unfortunately wore the same uniform, were just a bunch of sadistic pathetic creeps. The changed circumstances necessitated a hasty mental adjustment to future tactics.

An English padre greeted us – a saint in a dog collar! How is it that in a crisis you always seem to find a humble servant of God who can restore your faith in humanity by their selfless actions, and yet, in peacetime the church seems to consist of a lot of opinionated slobs?

Because we arrived late in the day, there were no official German rations for us, but the Yugoslav fellow-prisoners were very kind and fed us with potato soup and bread. They also distributed foul-smelling cigarettes, which, to many of my friends were more essential than food. In the middle of all this the Poles carried in a glider pilot whom the guards had shot dead for not going indoors during an air raid. I do not recall having been given any such warning but I could be mistaken.

I slept heavily that night but woke up the following morning with violent itching; an experience shared with everyone else. An examination of our bodies showed numerous bites in long straight lines – bedbugs, according to the experts. Being allergic to insect bites, mine were very large and inflamed, which brought forth the comment that mine must have worn clogs.

The makeshift pillowcase vest had to be cut off to conduct an effective 'search and destroy' foray against these loathsome bugs. By the time we were paraded for medical inspection my own morale was rock bottom, following a breakfast consisting of one mug of acorn coffee.

The primitive conditions in the camp hospital literally dropped my flagging spirits right through my frozen feet until they disappeared out of sight. Semi-naked men all round us with rubber pipes sticking out of their bodies, dripping with evil smelling pus. Others were having their wounds lanced with a kind of 'pull-through'. When it came to my turn I said that there was no point in undressing as I had only slight flesh wounds which had virtually healed up. On being asked why I had come to the hospital, I replied that the guards had brought me! It would seem that I had got mixed up with the wrong batch, would you please tell me (and the guards) where I am supposed to go next?

'No, I am not seriously wounded.'

'Yes, I am fit enough to transfer to an Oflag.' I was then directed to stand on one side, later on to be joined by other wounded officers who had heard my story and decided to seek a more hospitable prison.

We were marched back to our hut, names were taken, and then we were told to be ready to move out in a few hours time. Taking advantage of this break I tried to barter my few cigarettes, which the Yugoslavs had given to us the night before, for some additional clothing. They refused to take the cigarettes back but kindly provided a shirt, which was a vast improvement on the pillowcase, the remnants of which had been added to the rags on my bare feet.

As we were marched out of the camp we passed the Russian lager where the poor devils seemed to have no shelter and were standing in the open, rather like cows in a field. It vividly brought home to us how relatively lucky our own situation had been. In later years I discovered that the camp also housed Italian, French and American prisoners, in addition to the ones I had met personally – many, like the Polish women and children, on their way to an extermination camp.

Just prior to leaving the camp I heard my name being called and our Yugoslav contact tossed over the wire a pair of open-toed sandals, for which I could only wave my eternal gratitude. The mile-plus march down the hill to the railway station was no problem because I knew that the quicker we arrived, the sooner I would get my feet into footwear again, after twenty-three days of bare feet.

The first priority, assisted by friends, was to tear the remnants of the pillowcase into even smaller strips which were used to bandage my feet until the oversized sandals were a more reasonable fit. It felt fantastic to have soles again between me and mother earth although, if anything, my feet were not quite as warm as they had been.

After a long cold wait our train for Hanover arrived and we sat tightly wedged into the seats which, at least, ensured some mutual body warmth in the unheated carriage. Unfortunately, we missed our connection at Hanover where we received a very hostile reception from civilians on the platform. Having seen what our bombs had done to their city, it was easy to appreciate how they felt about the sight of enemy uniforms. The guards wasted no time in hustling us away to a Red Cross post where we received the first hot drink of the day.

We started the night in an air raid shelter, which was reasonably comfortable, and where we were able to pass the time away by playing cards. This only lasted an hour or so before we were turfed out to make room for civilians. (Hanover was a favourite target for our bombers in those days.) Our little force was evacuated to a platform waiting-room, where I spent one of the most miserable nights in my life. Not through any fear of bombs I hasten to add; that would have brought only blessed relief.

Possibly, it was a combination of the adrenalin wearing off following recovery from paralysis, coupled with delayed shock from my wounds. Silly as it sounds, the itching from the multiple bedbug bites was driving me crazy and, to crown it all, I discovered my left inner thigh, from crutch to knee, was painfully inflamed, presumably from a combination of ingrained dirt, friction, no underclothes and chapping from extreme cold.

The others were in a similar depressed mood. I missed the irrelevant banter and humour of the other-ranks, in whose company I had been up to now. When they have not got men to look after, officers just concentrate on keeping a stiff upper lip. Even the guards in their overcoats were feeling the cold and, when one of our party produced some tea leaves, they quickly found some hot water and mugs. It is surprising what benefit one can derive from a hot steaming cup of tea, no milk or sugar of course, just hot black tea.

Ultimately, our train arrived and we thankfully boarded it, forgetting all about Allied air attacks on trains moving in daylight. We just huddled together and fell asleep. When the train pulled in to Spangelburg-Kassel station around 2p.m. on 11 October, we were ushered into a warm room where, to our great surprise, hot drinks, sandwiches, cigarettes, apples and pears were served. We were now in the custody of the Oflag and were being treated as officers: they even brought us a glass of beer. To cast any doubt on the full enjoyment of this moment would be unfair to the efforts of our new custodians, but I did get a terrible guilt complex as I compared this with our previous experiences at Stalag XIB, under which some of my old wounded comrades would still be suffering.

I see from my diary that we did not leave the station until 7.25p.m., so we must have been there for over five hours awaiting transport. It did not seem as long as that, but time always flies when life is looking rosy. It was not a long drive because we arrived in the dark around 8.20p.m. at Oflag IX A/Z, situated at Rotenburg. Again, that lucky little fairy sitting on my shoulder had guided my destiny to full advantage because the Oflag was located in what had been a large prosperous school, standing in its own grounds, on the fringe of the beautiful Hartz mountains.

CHAPTER 4
Oflag IX A/Z

Unlike the majority of prisoners who lived in glorified Nissen huts, usually sited in a sea of mud, we could wander round under cover from room to room. The sleeping quarters were not unduly cramped, there was a separate dining-room, even a library and real flushing WCs. The camp had a huge central stairway right up to the top floor, with a central core down which the last suicide had plunged to his death shortly before our arrival.

Our reception in the entrance hall was a bit more formal than it had been at the station, but not really unfriendly. It was a full strip-search, coupled with a brief interrogation. I did not mind the interrogation, even adding REME to the standard rank, name and number query. Not much point in trying to conceal it in view of the large flashes on my shoulders.

Turning my pockets out was no great problem but it upset me when they confiscated my family photographs. This was still rankling when I moved on the strip stage, where even our bandages were removed to check for escape equipment which was always issued to troops like us before any operation. I had completely forgotten about mine because the map and money had been hidden in my smock, which had been cut off and discarded when my wounds had first been dressed, nearly a month ago. Suddenly, I remembered that I had hidden the compass in the lining of my red beret which was perched on my head!

I took off my battledress blouse first, knowing that they would give it a thorough search, tossed my beret casually on to the table, and threw my shirt on top of it. Whilst I was taking my trousers

The family photographs that were confiscated by the Germans. The first shows the author with his mother; the second with his fiancée, Muriel

off, another young guard moved over and examined the shirt minutely, presumably because it was not standard British army issue. My trousers quickly followed the other clothing, again ensuring that they covered the beret which had still not been examined. Then, they found 'IT'.

The guard's grunt of satisfaction as he found the packet, carefully concealed in the lining of my trousers, brought the NCO in charge of the searchers quickly on the scene. Then I remembered what they had found. A major problem if you are trying to escape is how to carry water; access to drinking water is usually restricted and, when available, it is sensible to carry some away, as well as drinking your fill. A wartime condom, being much thicker and stronger than its present day counterpart can hold a substantial quantity of water without splitting; in every sense it was an efficient dual purpose addendum to your military equipment. The small internal pocket in the trouser lining did not interfere with any military function.

I found afterwards that all the other prisoners had surrendered theirs at the previous 'empty your pockets' stage – I just forgot it was there. When the guards realised what they had found it became apparent that they only viewed it from a conventional user viewpoint, because heavy Teutonic humour followed – made even more complicated because the NCO had to translate the young German guard's jibes into English, and my responses back into German.

My own recent events closely followed my father's pattern in the first world war, as he also finished up as a wounded POW. The stories he told me about his own prisoner of war experiences now bore me in good stead. During a war the psychology of both governments is to exaggerate the enemy's shortcomings so as to turn ordinary citizens into professional killers, which was not very helpful when you found yourself their prisoner. However, my father's exposé of their character and sense of humour was now worth its weight in gold. The repartee now went something like this:

'Ha! Ha! you will not be wanting this; you will not be finding any women here.'

'I know there are none now but I was going to write to Father Christmas to put one in my stocking.'

'Ha! Ha! Father Christmas, Ha! Ha!, Hans did you hear that? No, no, you will not require it.'

'In that case please accept it as a gift from me and *****'.

They found this excruciatingly funny. I saw the officer in charge of reception start to move towards us, so I signalled to the guards with my eyes, scooped up my beret and all my clothes, and dutifully moved on to the next stage which was an intimate body search. The guards here had enjoyed the joking and accepted my statement that my spinal wound did not allow me to bend over so I got away lightly. We then passed through a doorway into the welcoming hands of our own medical staff, one of whom threw a blanket round my naked body, whilst another relieved me of my clothing.

A major standing nearby started to reprimand me for fraternising with the search party, but as soon as it dawned on me what he was saying, I blew up. To me he represented the stupid 'blimps' who had made such a mess of our relief at Arnhem which had resulted in such a tragic loss of lives, apart from my own incapacity. As my temper took over, I have no clear recollection of what I said. One witness told me later that it was very basic but sexually quite impossible. Another one asked if I had been a sergeant-major before I was commissioned, as only warrant officers could command such a non-stop flow of invective.

I regained control of myself just as quickly as I had lost it, turned on my heels and followed the two orderlies to a heaven on earth in the prison hospital.

The next few days were spent in a state of heavenly bliss which words just cannot describe. In retrospect, it was apparent that I had been running on emergency reserve strength for some time and had now reached the point of total collapse. Indeed, many of my fellow prisoners left in Stalag IXB died there over the next few weeks as a result of the poor environment and lack of medical attention. It is more than likely that I would have shared the same fate if I had not conned my way out of it. As it was, as soon as I arrived in the hospital ward the blanket was whisked off, and my fellow inmates and I were left to soak in large portable zinc baths aligned down the centre of the ward; what bliss as the waist-deep hot water soaked into our filthy bodies.

The staff were all versed in mass receptions, one orderly starting at the end of the row washing our hair, eyes, nose, ears, etc., down to our shoulders, before drying us off. Two more orderlies followed him and, whilst we stood up in the bath they gave every square inch of our bodies a thorough cleansing. We were dried off by yet another medic before a couple of doctors examined and dressed our wounds, bedbug bites and sores of various sizes. Then, into warm flannel pyjamas, before being tucked-up in a proper hospital bed.

After a hot meal I stretched out and gazed round the brightly lit ward into which no bedbug would even dare to show itself. I absorbed the essence of kindness pervading the atmosphere and fell into a deep relaxing sleep.

I slept solidly for the next two days, only waking up to eat and perform the minimum of activities. Everyone was fitted out with underwear, shirts, socks, English soap and razors, so I was able to enjoy the first decent shave for a month. A padre appeared with a supply of blank POW letter cards, which he showed us how to fill in. He would not accept any delay. I was only too glad to get some news home, but one or two wanted to leave it until they had caught up with their sleep. He stood his ground until he had at least one card from each of the new intake before dashing away to ensure that the letters received priority with the German censors.

Even the German Camp Commandant was considerate: although we had arrived on the Wednesday, it was Saturday before he paid us a visit to outline the rules and regulations of the Oflag.

There was a beam-type weighing machine in the yard on which I weighed myself and was horrified to find that two stone had disappeared in the last month. No matter how many times I tried the scales they would not go above 133 pounds. I stripped off to check on the bites and sores in front of a mirror, before hastily putting my pyjamas back on again. It was easier to accept the low reading on the weighing machine after seeing the wasted figure in the mirror.

The doctor advised us to start walking around as soon as we felt like it, so I got dressed in what I thought was a brand new battledress. It was my own battledress which had been sewn up, but how on earth they had cleaned it so professionally I shall never know. Even the blood-stains on the pocket linings were hardly visible. This was my first experience of what a POW camp can do, with very little resources but an abundance of enthusiasm, labour and time. Fully dressed again, even to boots and gaiters, I had an overwhelming desire to go somewhere, a wish difficult to satisfy in the confines of a POW camp; I contented myself by walking across the yard into the main prison block to attend the first of many camp concerts.

Prisoners have to be wary that their captors do not infiltrate spies into the camp to pass on information regarding escape plans etc. We had all received various cross-checks and vetting, but I think I was the first to be cleared – REME personnel were well known across all units, so many people were able to confirm my UK status. Others were not so fortunate and had to undergo extensive vetting before they finally received their security clearance.

On the following day a padre gave us Holy Communion in the ward. A corporal gave us a short back and sides; in view of the fact that it was six weeks since I had had my last haircut, I was beginning to feel like a violinist. After our wounds had been redressed I sat down to write to a long letter to my fiancée Muriel, and fill in my YMCA diary from the heterogeneous scraps of paper and empty cigarette packets which I had been using for writing.

On Tuesday 17 October, one day short of the month since I was wounded, I attended a repatriation medical examination by German doctors. The purpose of this was to exchange seriously wounded prisoners from both sides through the auspices of the Red Cross. I had entered my name for repatriation, not because I thought there was any possibility of succeeding, but simply because I was getting a bit frustrated with our British doctors who insisted that I could not have a bullet 'in that hole', 'because you would be dead'. When I responded by asking them what had caused the hole, all I got was the possibility of a non-penetrating piece of shrapnel, but no bullet, 'otherwise, you would be dead'.

The repatriation board seemed to be a good opportunity to get a second opinion. All went well until the German doctor told me to bend over so that he could examine my wound more easily. I recovered consciousness to find myself in a different bed and ward, surrounded by doctors who immediately started to carry out movement tests on my legs and body.

Apparently, the German doctor shared the cynicism of his British counterparts, and as I bent over, he tapped the wound. The bullet must have touched something vital because I passed out. He was most apologetic and I was most conciliatory because one of the first things he said was, that he would arrange to have me X-rayed to ascertain what was inside.

This turned out to be one of the highlights of my sojourn in the Oflag as it necessitated going into the adjacent town of Rotenburg. It was some considerable time before I found out that a shortage of transport kept postponing the visit. Having found out how far the hospital was from the camp, I suggested that it would be within walking distance, so long as I could rest periodically. This was agreed, subject to the standard condition of swearing on oath that I would not attempt to escape, would make no preparations to escape at a later date or assist anyone else to escape.

It was a nice crisp day when my elderly guard and I stepped outside the confines of the camp and strolled towards the town. The guard flung his rifle across his shoulder knowing full well that, even if I did escape, there would be a court martial waiting for me back in the UK for breaking my oath. The British authorities were, quite rightly, insistent that we could not break this oath, whatever the circumstances, as it would have immediate repercussions on thousands of other prisoners.

As soon as we were out of sight of the prison, I got the signal which I had anticipated: would I give him a cigarette? When he saw the full packet and realised that I did not smoke, I had no difficulty in dictating the slow pace and frequent rests to take in the new surroundings. The civilian population showed no hostility and we stopped on a few occasions for a chat, mostly with his friends, but several times with girls who shared the international fascination of females for any man in a different uniform.

We reached a small square where the guard found some close friends, so we all sat down in the winter sunshine. I offered my cigarettes all round, which seemed a good way to delay the time for departure whilst I enjoyed the scenery. It had the opposite effect because, as soon as they had lit up, we headed across the square. Our destination turned out to be a small café where our new hosts insisted on buying cups of acorn coffee for us, my taste buds having now adjusted to its flavour. The waitress produced a plate of small cakes of indefinable origin, which tasted much better than they looked.

By now, my friends were leaning back in their chairs in a near state of mental intoxication as they inhaled genuine tobacco smoke for the first time in many years. My request for a toilet merely brought a jerk of the head to one end of the room, but, as I stood hesitating which way to go, the waitress appeared and escorted me to the 'little boy's' room. On impulse I gave her a bar of soap before opening the door of the urinal. When I emerged she was waiting for me and signalled for me to remain there until she returned. She disappeared and returned a short time later with some of the cakes wrapped up in newspaper which I stowed in my battledress blouse.

I must have been away from the guard for quite a long time, but he showed no signs of concern, indeed he was becoming an important person because our presence in the café had attracted a little crowd, including the last two girls who had tried to chat us up. It suddenly dawned on me from the few words I understood and his gestures, that he was telling them that I was a wounded para officer captured at Arnhem whom he was escorting to the hospital. I was not too happy about this revelation, but he knew his audience and soon I was the centre of attention.

It is not generally known in the UK that the Germans lavished more praise and publicity on the stand at Arnhem than even the British media. Everyone felt my wings and insignia; the girls tried on my beret for size with the guard having to intervene to get it back off them. In the meantime the guard was having a whale of a time; he was, I think, refighting Arnhem. I could not tell what line he was shooting, but it obviously raised my esteem with his small audience to such an extent that the girls' flirtatious fraternization was completely ignored. The local population knew that their Oflag held some of the 'Red Devils', but I must have been the first one to be seen in the flesh.

All good things must come to an end; the guard probably

realised that we were in danger of missing our appointment, because we suddenly rushed away at high speed, straight to the hospital. I think my guess was right because there was a lot of waving of arms, the usual shouting and pointing to the clock. This called for my Thespian role, so, without being asked, I subsided into a chair and adopted a weary haggard look. This did the trick; the guard obviously inferred that he had brought me as fast as was physically possible. The heated discussion ended as quickly as it started and we all retired to a small room containing an X-ray machine.

When I put the cakes from the café inside my battledress blouse I had completely forgotten that I would be getting undressed and, as soon as the parcel came to light, it came as a surprise to see the guard pick it up and open it. The nurse did not waste any time; as soon as I was stripped off she had me on the table, then she and the guard disappeared behind the screen whilst the plate was exposed. She bustled out of the room and said something to the guard as she disappeared through the door. This must have been to stop me putting my clothes on again because, when I tried to do this, he shook his head and took my underpants out of my hand.

The room was not really warm enough to stand around in your birthday suit, and it was a relief when the nurse reappeared with someone who was obviously a doctor holding a wet X-ray in his hand. He was kind enough to show it to me and knew enough English to explain that really, I should be dead! I was a bit wary when he said he wanted to examine me in view of what had happened last time, but I was in no position to refuse. It turned out to be nothing more than medical curiosity. The guard held the still-wet plate at my side whilst the doctor and nurse tried to evaluate how the bullet had got into that position without killing me *en route*. I received the best logical explanation of my wound from that obscure doctor in a little cottage hospital in Rotenburg than all the other specialists put together.

We had arrived to abuse for being late for our appointment but we left amidst general cordiality. Unfortunately, we had to rush back, as presumably the guard realised that we had wasted too much time on the outward journey. There was, however, still another pleasant surprise for me: when I visited the loo in the hospital, before retracing steps back to the camp, the guard produced my packet of cakes, now broken down into small parcels, and showed me how to hide them!

When we arrived back at the prison they did give me a very superficial search which would certainly have discovered the cakes in their original hiding place. They did not, however, find any in their new location. It had been quite a red-letter day; I had made a useful contact with a guard and, what is more, we both trusted each other; the medical staff had enough after-dinner miracle escape facts to keep them happy, the café clientele could describe what a genuine Arnhem soldier looked like, the waitress could enjoy the luxury of decent soap and I could only wonder at the fairy-stories the two girls would give to their friends.

Our guards were mostly from older generations; the best in my eyes were those who had been British POWs in the First World War. The German authorities must have felt that these men, too old for overseas active service, would make ideal guards as they knew all the tricks. They did, but many of them were secret father figures to men of my age – the same vintage as their own sons fighting all over Europe. They were not disloyal to the Reich, but at the same time, they could be sympathetic to our needs. I recall that one of them was overwhelmed with the genuine sympathy offered by his prisoners when news of his son's death on the Russian front became known.

Fortunately, the same group of guards stayed with us until the end. There were some younger guards of our own age group, on temporary attachment until their wounds healed up. They were no real problem; all they were concerned with was maximising their own personal relaxation when off duty before returning to active duty. There were the usual 'creeps' who exist in every society throughout the world. Men who would sell their own mother into a brothel to save their own skins. During a war they usually find a safe haven, well away from the bullets: we had our fair share of them. One parole walk was ruined by the antics of one of these creeps, presumably trying to make himself indispensable to the security of the Oflag. He went right to the top of our black list, so we laid our plans.

The next time he went on any form of roving party, which turned out to be a wood-cutting party, he again excelled himself by being as obstructive as possible. However, our stay-at-home colleagues had been on the look-out for him and knew exactly what to do. A delegation went to see the German Security Officer to make a formal complaint that officers who volunteered for manual labour under the parole system to try and keep the Oflag warm, should not be subjected to blackmail intimidation for the personal gratification of their guards.

On our return the guards were all searched. Nothing incriminating was found on any of them except the 'creep'. He could not explain away two packets of cigarettes hidden in the lining of his overcoat. He disappeared from the scene, hopefully to a front line somewhere. Equally important was the fact that the German authorities never found out how they had been manipulated. The 'creep' was probably more unpopular with his fellow guards than he was with us: they dared not put a foot wrong for fear of his reporting them to the powers that be. This had dried up all their illegal 'goodies' to which they, and their wives, had become accustomed. We had no scruples in involving them in our deception: we had little choice in the matter. When the 'creep' left his overcoat whilst he answered a call of nature, the other guards stared intently in the direction we had suggested, so that they could honestly say they had seen nothing. We did not have to tell any lies because the authorities preferred to hush things up.

Hunger was with us night and day. Occasionally, on the wood-cutting parties, we might temporarily assuage it for an hour or so, but it soon returned. The new arrivals tried to emulate the old 'kriegies' who chewed each mouthful to excess before swallowing it. I found it impossible to eat and talk at the same time. At the first appraisal this would appear to be the best course of action to spin a meal out. It did not work for me. If I was engaged in conversation during a meal, I would suddenly discover that I had eaten my food without noticing it. Therefore, I tried to avoid conversation in order that I might count a required number of chewing actions before swallowing the minuscule portion of food in my mouth. This worked until someone engaged me in conversation – then I was back to square one!

Chocolate demanded the greatest discipline. I used to put a minute piece in my mouth every ten laps of the quadrangle and see how long I could hold on to the flavour. I think we only had one two-ounce bar every month: it was one commodity I found it impossible to ration. It probably took me several hours of continuous walking to eat one small bar. I never tried to eat chocolate and talk; if someone joined me on my perambulations I was strong-willed enough to stop eating when engaged in conversation; to do anything else would have been fatal. The consumption of chocolate demanded total undivided attention to flavour and memory. This habit has been with me ever since.

On one occasion we were all treated to a small noggin of real rot-gut whisky which had been tenderly distilled by its devoted band of converted alcoholics. It made a pleasant change, but I cannot claim that I missed alcoholic drinks. However, I am jumping several weeks ahead, so back to the time of the repatriation board.

Following my collapse, I was kept in the 'critical' ward for a fortnight, before being allowed back to the 'convalescent' wing and finally being transferred to the main block on 3 November, the day before my birthday.

My twenty-fourth birthday was celebrated by eating a 2oz bar of plain 'York' chocolate in one sitting! The living quarters were far superior to the majority of POW camps, mine was a relatively large room, probably a pre-war classroom, with double tiered bunk beds around all four walls, with tables and chairs down the centre. There were (I think) two windows with radiators under each one on which we dried our washing and tea leaves.

The straw-filled mattresses were supported on transverse loose boards, many of which, over the years, had been commandeered for escape purposes; it was necessary to adjust the remaining few with great care to ensure that you did not fall through the bed.

Initially, because I had just been released from hospital, I was given a bottom bunk, but, later on I changed it for a top one because this gave a better sense of freedom. I found the lower bunks quite claustrophobic although, funnily enough, most people seemed to prefer them.

My room, No. 237, held an amiable cross-section of several nationalities, including quite a few Canadians who played poker every night with monotonous regularity. My closest room-mate was a major from New Zealand.

There really was no excuse for boredom as the camp was extremely well organised. There were men with a wide range of skills and professions, all of whom were only too glad to acquire pupils to lecture. The first subject I concentrated on was the calorific value of various foods, the properties of vitamins and their sources. At this stage of the war parcels were not getting through from the UK. I certainly did not receive one of the many despatched by my family. However, there were residual stocks of Red Cross parcels which were carefully rationed out. Most people traded in their Red Cross rations for their own particular preference, for example, honey for jam or vice versa.

My policy was quite simple. I had carefully evaluated the weight and calorific value of each item of Red Cross food, and only exchanged when the food on offer had a greater calorific value than mine. Taste bud preference was completely ignored. Normally, the Canadians would not exchange their peanut butter to which they seemed addicted, but even they succumbed to exchanging it for cigarettes when supplies of the latter started to dry up.

The bread ration was issued on a daily basis and the drill here was to save some each day to build up a reserve stock. When a day's ration was accumulated it was exchanged for a two day slab, and so on until your required emergency ration was all in one

Cooking vessel

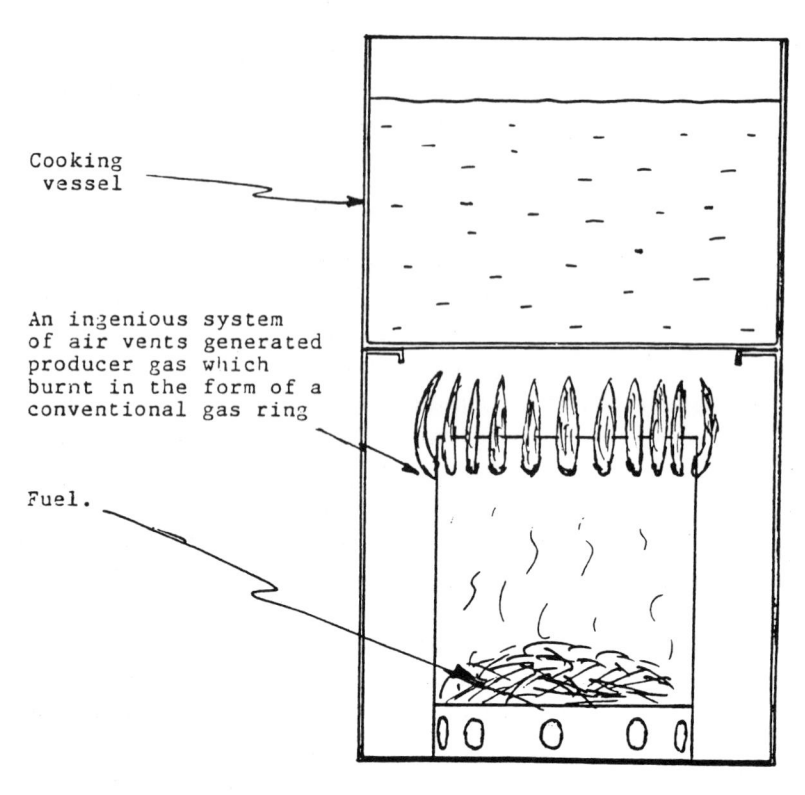

An ingenious system of air vents generated producer gas which burnt in the form of a conventional gas ring

Fuel.

The Kriegie cooker used by POWs was manufactured mainly from 'Klim' tins – dried milk tins. It was a most remarkable and efficient little cooker which we used to make tea, and also to boil up nettle leaves etc. Scraps of paper and a few slithers of wood were all that was necessary to fuel it.

piece of loaf. By this time it was hardening off with age and lasted much longer when chewing it.

It took considerable willpower to ignore the food stock against the perpetual hunger pains we were all suffering from. We tried to alleviate this by drinking fluids to excess: a full bladder helped to ameliorate the ache of hunger. Constantly overloaded bladders necessitated frequent visits to the urinal, a habit which persisted with me for many years afterwards.

The limited ration of tea leaves would only permit about one cup of unsweetened black tea per day, a ration completely inadequate to meet our high liquid intake requirements, so after first use, the tea leaves were dried-out on top of the radiators for subsequent multiple brews. It was only when the anaemic-looking tea leaves refused to colour the water in which they were boiled, that they were reluctantly consigned to the waste bin.

These personal brew-ups were achieved in a remarkable piece of POW engineering: a small home-made 'Kriegie' cooker, which could boil a mug of tea on scraps of paper, a few twigs or slithers of wood from the bunk boards. It also served for cooking nettles and dandelion roots collected whilst gardening or on parole walk. Unfortunately, I never manufactured one myself, having had one donated, in order that my craftsman skills could concentrate on other activities requested by the escape committee. Thus, the finer details of construction have escaped my memory, even though I used it hundreds of times. It was probably the most efficient little cooker I have ever come across and relegates the current armed forces solid metal model into obsolescence.

Prisoners were issued with their own individual bread ration – plus jam, when this was available, either from German or Red Cross sources, but the main food supplies were bulked together and we ate in mess groups. The cooks deserve full credit for the tasty meals which they managed to produce from such restricted ingredients: a far cry from our recollections of army catering in England.

The camp had its fair share of Thespians; their acting and costumes were brilliant and they kept us entertained with a much appreciated variety of shows. I went to every one, not just once but every time I could get a seat. Similarly, the film shows, which were a mixture of English and German, were either instructive or entertaining; it was very rare to find a dud. Attitudes to entertainment depended a lot on how long each individual had been in captivity and their evaluation of the military situation. Some of the longer-serving prisoners had sunk into mental lethargy, with no optimism in their hearts for an early release, whilst others of the same vintage were ridiculously optimistic.

The majority of the new airborne intake had been wounded

POW entertainment – *A Midsummer's Night Dream*

and were concentrating on getting back into good physical shape. We accepted, without question, the advice given by the experts, that escape during the bleak German winter was not practicable. In view of our recent wide knowledge of the progress on all war fronts, it was confidently anticipated that it would all be over before the next winter. If anything had gone wrong then, I think the late summer of 1945 would have seen mass 'airborne' escape attempts from the Oflags.

The camp had its own illegal wireless set so that we got frequent updates from the BBC regarding progress of the war. This news was given out on a room-by-room basis by a member of the wireless team, under very strict security arrangements. There is a note in my diary that a rendering of 'Ave Maria' on the German wireless made a great impression on me. Although I can vaguely recall the occasion, I cannot remember where the German wireless was located. In any event, not being able to understand the German announcer, it would not have had much interest for me but the 'Ave Maria' obviously did.

Boredom was the unseen enemy of all Oflag inmates. Our troops in the Stalags were made to work; they had plenty to occupy themselves with – by doing the minimum amount of work they could get away with, whilst taking advantage of every opportunity to scrounge extra food. As a result, the suicide rate among other ranks was much smaller than that in the Oflags. The majority of officers developed their own particular daily routine to combat lethargy and boredom. One thing we all had in common was not to get out of bed until the very last minute for the early morning roll-call (*appelle*). It was far preferable to lie in the relative warmth of your bed half asleep, than hang around in the cold which seemed to emphasize the hunger pangs.

The ultimate development of this policy was to fling sufficient warm clothes on top of your pyjamas, go on parade at the last moment, and, after roll-call, undress, wash and shave, etc, prior to getting dressed for the day's activities. As the weather got colder and colder, so the bizarre styles of dress became more unmilitary. All roll-calls were carried out in the quadrangle, and even though

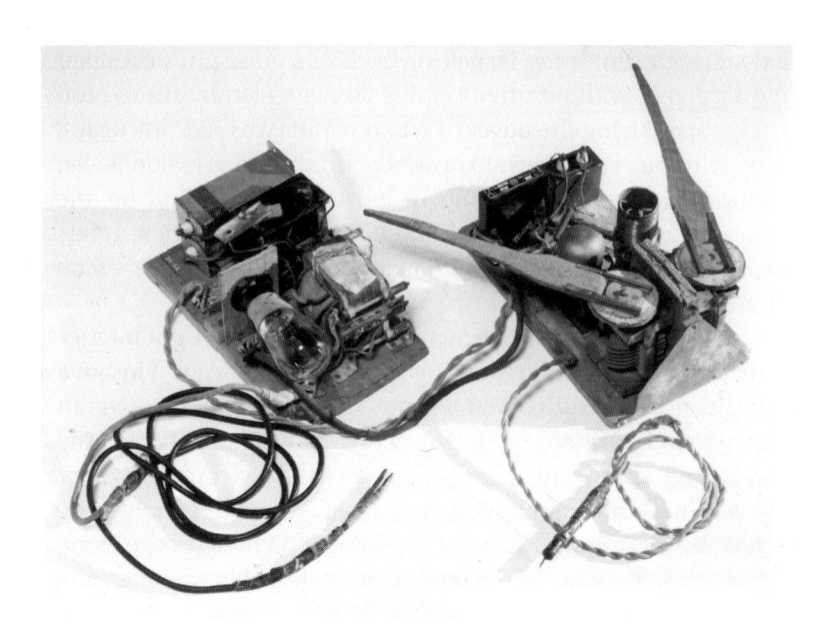

POW camp radio now in Imperial War Museum

the guards did not usually protract the head count, by the time they finished we were quite cold.

The longer-serving prisoners had a much wider wardrobe than the airborne intake; we, by comparison, looked quite military, simply because we had no option. They, on the other hand, produced balaclavas, head scarves, fur-trimmed hats etc, which made them look a 'right shower' as we all reluctantly oozed out of the building each morning to line up in the freezing cold. This clearly offended the German military mind and several dire warnings were given about the required standard of military attire for the morning roll-calls. These had the opposite effect, of course.

When the final warning was received, everyone organised their own fancy dress for the next parade. Time dims the memory but the sequence of events was something like this: first of all, a squad of immaculately dressed officers obeyed the commands of one of their party and marched in Guards' style, with exaggerated arm and leg movements, to their position on the parade ground; the

Germans beamed at this transformation, but their faces dropped when the remainder of the Oflag marched just as smartly on parade: their style of headgear ranged right across the centuries, all beautifully fashioned from newspaper, Napoleonic style, Cavalier, high-peak, etc; uniforms were equally imaginative, the funniest were the Scotch kilts consisting of folded blankets wrapped round and secured with safety-pins, adorned with a wide range of sporrans ranging from funny to pornographic.

One thing was common to all the squads: the standard of marching which, with its drill and loud commands would have delighted a Sandhurst sergeant-major. Unfortunately, the overall 'military' effect was spoilt as each squad varied its step from the slow march through intermediate speeds to a light infantry gallop. The Germans were furious and really blew their tops. Time went on and on as we progressively froze, but everyone agreed that this had been the best goon-baiting episode for a long time. The outcome was a truce: we improved our standards of dress and the Germans kept the duration of the roll-call to an absolute minimum. In extreme weather conditions they even condescended to hold them indoors, so our efforts were well worthwhile.

My daily routine started each morning by taking Holy Communion, having become very friendly with a padre who only had a small regular congregation. Early on, I did a lot of reading until my eyes started to play tricks; this was, apparently, attributable to my poor physical condition and it disappeared when I was able to enjoy a normal diet again. Daily walking exercise around the yard was controlled on a time duration basis, the laps being far too small to keep a numerical tally.

The schools' ablutions that we used were located in the basement, so that washing and shaving could be carried out in relative comfort. We even had the luxury of a hot shower every now and again, the first of which turned out to be a disaster. Nobody had warned us that the water was only turned on for one minute so that all newcomers were caught in the lather stage, which had to be washed off with freezing cold water over a sink, to the annoyance of the guards: they controlled input and output to the few showers with the same efficiency that a farmer controls his cows in the milking parlour. The conventional routine was to pre-lather yourself in cold water so as to enjoy the full minute washing it off in hot water.

There was a rather disconcerting incident in December: I was performing my ablutions and suddenly everything went silent. I looked round to find out why everybody had stopped talking and was shaken to see their mouths still moving, but, not a whisper of noise was reaching me. I hastily dried myself and went over to the medical room, where large quantities of oil were poured into each ear before sealing them with cotton-wool. The doctor did not seem too concerned and I gathered it was a common occurrence. Spending forty-eight hours in a state of complete deafness was yet another experience which made me appreciate the outlook of other less fortunate people who have such disabilities on a permanent basis.

At the appointed time I presented myself to the MI room, where an orderly held a large kidney bowl under each ear whilst the doctor syringed them. I thought they had washed my brains out; even the slightest whisper was deafening. The quantity of foreign matter floating in the bowl defied belief that there was sufficient space in the ears to accommodate it. It turned out to be debris from the Oosterbeek first-aid post which had fallen on us as the plaster above was shattered with bullets and mortar bombs. Under normal conditions the ear wax would carry it out, but my ears were so full that nature could not cope. I had been washing my ears when the deafness hit me; this must have moved the large ball of accumulated wax and dirt to cut off the sound. For the next day or so I wore cotton-wool in my ears, until they could withstand the sounds of normal life.

As soon as I felt strong enough I volunteered to work in the camp vegetable garden, which was located on the other side of the security fence. It was the wrong time of the year to enjoy the mental freedom of being on the other side of the wire, but I made the most of it. All we had to do was to give our parole and then potter in the garden without even a guard standing over us. Minimum security was covered by guards in the overhead towers glancing occasionally in our direction.

My diary records that we were digging and collecting leeks just before Christmas, replanting rhubarb in mid-March and, ultimately, planting two rows of lettuce seeds only six days before we abandoned camp. All produce from the garden went into the communal pot, but this did not apply to dandelions and nettles which could be retained for our consumption; I can confidently guarantee that there was not a single dandelion or nettle root left in that garden when we evacuated camp.

Christmas and New Year were celebrated in style. Perhaps the Christmas atmosphere was a little muted; after all, it is normally a family celebration and we were a long way from our loved ones. No such inhibitions for New Year; everyone felt this was the beginning of the year when we would be free again and it was celebrated really well. The party started gently with a gramophone recital of records covering all tastes. This was followed by a long news reading: the news at this stage was not good but the BBC was playing it down. We thought the Ardennes offensive was a last desperate fling on the part of the Germans – if we had known the true facts, our celebrations would have been a little muted.

Dinner was probably the most substantial meal we ever enjoyed in the Oflag. Toad-in-the-hole, mashed potatoes, creamed leeks (which I had helped to dig out of the garden a few days earlier), pudding and liquor sauce. With an unusual feeling of plenty in our stomachs, we then enjoyed an entertaining show called 'New Year's Follies', perfectly balanced to match our current optimistic view on life. The show lasted from 10.15p.m. to 12.15a.m., with an interval when Horlicks was served. The night's entertainment finished with a rousing rendering of 'God Save the King', before 'lights out' came all too quickly at 12.30a.m.

When we woke the following morning it seemed as though the previous night had been an illusion, but we soon realised that it was not when we had real porridge for breakfast accompanied by

Best Wishes for
CHRISTMAS 1944
AND THE NEW YEAR

OFLAG IX A/Z. Germany.

1944 Christmas card from Oflag IX A/Z

tea with sugar and milk! I went back to bed so that I could stretch out for the first time in months without suffering pangs of hunger. On a note of pessimism we thought it must be all over, but no, lunch turned out to be a glorious repast of eggs and potatoes, followed by an entertaining quiz during the afternoon. After this we flooded the ice rink and held an ice-skating meeting before finishing off the day's entertainment with a gramophone recital of 'swing'. It was with sheer utter disbelief that we sat down to an evening meal of fish and cheese, potatoes, fruit salad and coffee!

On the following day we had our first parole walk in the afternoon; so our German captors had certainly joined in the spirit of the New Year celebration. Full credit must be given to everyone who had organised these celebrations. To an outsider reading this, it must appear a little ludicrous to starve yourself in order to enjoy one glorious blow-out, but anyone who has been in our situation will appreciate the mental and morale uplift which it can engender.

The celebrations put us in a relaxed mood to enjoy the skating on the DIY rink in the schoolyard, plus the parole walks, which were on a larger scale than the garden fatigue parties, but on a similar basis. Individual paroles had to be given regarding not escaping, followed by a walk in the adjacent countryside under a small guard escort.

CHAPTER 5

The Outside World

The parole walks were very agreeable but not as good as the wood-cutting parties: the building's central heating system was suffering from a shortage of fuel, which left us very cold with no food inside us to combat it. Negotiations were carried out at a high level with the Germans to allow officers to volunteer for wood-cutting duties, with all the logs coming back to our camp and not supplementing the German war effort. My name was one of the first to go down on the list; these outings were to be the best I enjoyed as a POW. It was the usual drill: parole, followed by a very small guard escort party to areas in the woods, much further away from the camp than our slow-moving parole walks ever took us.

The Germans provided us with a horse and cart to carry the logs back to the Oflag and we filled this to the brim with long logs, on the basis that there was no point in cutting the logs smaller as we did not know the size the boiler could take. In any case the saws were blunt and needed sharpening. This left more time to relax. We never returned before the deadline, irrespective of how much work we did or did not do. Our guards were in no hurry to get back to base because this automatically severed the tobacco and cigarettes which we rationed to them. The longer they stayed away from camp the more baccy they could beg off us.

It was not long before we realised the potential to open up a new black market, not with the guards, who were generally quite old and had limited opportunities to match our requirements, but with farms in the vicinity. One of my friends spoke fluent

German, so when the four guards had ensconced themselves in their usual alert position around a blazing fire, brewing-up their acorn coffee and smoking our cigarettes, we wandered at will in the trees and approached them with a proposition. We wanted to search for a black market source – under escort, of course, but it was necessary that all four guards agreed to this and shared our baccy rewards, because we did not want to get any of them in trouble with their superiors. It was a question of all or none.

Whilst they argued this amongst themselves I produced an unopened packet of cigarettes, which brought the conversation to an abrupt halt. Their reply was to the effect that this area was fairly new to them, but 'Yes!' they would accept our terms. They knew there was a large farm in 'that direction' because some of the camp food came from it; they would do their best to find it but could not guarantee success.

We accepted the terms and three of us set off for this potential food store, my friend and I and just one guard. It turned out to be not too far, perhaps half-an-hour's walk away. I was not prepared in the slightest for what we found. It was just as though we had walked onto another planet. We emerged from the trees into a large field of turnips which was in the process of being harvested by a totally female labour force, numbering about twenty, under the control of a single guard.

There was nothing wrong with the farm buildings in the distance or the very neat and efficient cultivation all round us, or even the guard muffled up in his overcoat. He was about our own age and probably a wounded veteran having a working convalescence before returning to the front line. It was the labour force which horrified us: young females whose faces were haggard beyond their years, their pitiful clothing completely inadequate for the cold winter weather. They were filthy, with dirty unkempt hair and their scratching showed that they were all entertaining lice.

It was hard to comprehend how the girls we remembered back in England could be sisters-in-name to these poor creatures. Although their physical appearance shook us to our cores, it was their eyes which were the ultimate horror: blank, unseeing, without any expression; these skeletons were just like zombies from outer space. This was our first contact with slave labour and we just could not comprehend the horror of it all.

Our guard soon had things sorted out with the new guard. He was, after all, old enough to be our father and he adopted a parental negotiating role between my friend and the girls' guard. The three chatted away in German whilst they fixed the price in cigarettes for turnips; I, having sweetened the new guard with a couple of cigarettes, kept the opened packet in my hand, ready to hand out the agreed barter quantity.

I could not keep my eyes off the girls and had lost all interest in the food negotiations as I tried to force the horror of the scene into my brain, which seemed reluctant to accept the evidence of my eyes.

My friend was a very hard bargainer and secured the maximum quantity of turnips which we could carry for a relatively modest number of cigarettes. I started to shuffle the required cigarettes out of the packet when the young guard said something to me, which brought a prompt reply from my friend. I asked what he had said and received an equally prompt reply. My interest in the girls had been misinterpreted by the young guard, who now offering me any woman of my choice for the remaining two or three cigarettes in the packet.

The two old guards looked quite bemused at the furious argument which followed between the two Englanders when I closed the packet and handed it to the young guard. Ignoring my friend's vehement protests, I pointed to a girl whose eyes still appeared to have a flicker of life in them before we walked behind the waiting horse and cart for some privacy. This was thirty or forty yards from where we had been standing and, as we walked over, I tried to engage her in conversation. This was difficult because she walked behind me like a dog, with her eyes cast down on the ground. She spoke a language which was new to me; it could have been one of the east European countries, as all I could decipher was that it was not French, German, Dutch or Polish in which I had picked up the odd word or phrase.

There was some embarrassment when we reached concealment because she knew why she was there. She could not understand my protests with one hand, whilst I fumbled for a bar of chocolate in my pocket with the other one. Her eyes lit up when she realised that the chocolate was for her; I fed it to her in small pieces, in case she gulped it down. I need not have worried, because she realised my intentions were not what she thought they were, and I watched a flicker of life come back into her eyes as she rolled the chocolate round her mouth before swallowing it.

In spite of my overwhelming pity for her, I still had a horror of her lice and ensured that we kept a safe distance from each other. I hope she interpreted this as a symbol of the purity of my intentions!

Halfway through the small bar of chocolate, I passed the remainder to her, which, to my surprise she did not eat; instead, she concealed it in a pocket hidden inside her skirt. With sign language I indicated that I understood that she wanted to save it for later on; in reply, she pointed to the other girls, and then I realised she was saving it for her friend. I was choked; it brought home to me vividly how, in the midst of man's inhumanity to man, virtue cannot be totally extinguished. How anyone in her physical condition could think about sharing her chocolate with a friend was, at that stage of my life, beyond comprehension. I emptied my pockets of all my remaining black market goodies, cigarettes and soap; unfortunately, there was no more chocolate, as the other bar had been intended for my own once-a-month treat.

Having no trust in her guard, who would most certainly confiscate it, she hid what she could in the 'gamekeeper' pockets of her skirt. We then hid the remaining items in the framework of the cart: she seemed confident that it would be safe there. She straightened up, said something which I could not understand before looking me straight in the eyes – they said it all – then she turned away and walked back to her workforce in the field. I followed her a few seconds later, pretending to button up my clothing, to the satisfaction of the two guards and the equal disapproval of my friend.

He took a lot of convincing, and it was only when he discovered that I had parted with all my treasure trove of black market goodies that he started to weaken. The discovery that I had also parted with my precious chocolate bar, finally convinced him that I had acted as an officer and gentleman. The episode left a permanent scar in my memory and, although it still gives my conscience a warm feeling to recall it, the awful memory of those zombie eyes will stay with me for the remainder of my days. Later on we met other groups of slave workers, but none of them were in the physical state of that initial group.

On the basis that it might lead to further opportunities, I made adverse comments on the sharpness of the saws with which we had been provided, and offered to sharpen them. Much to my surprise, this offer was taken up and I found myself in what might have been the school gardener's shed, armed with a blade setting wrench, a blunt saw file, a hammer and a screw driver. These were counted out to me in such a manner that I knew there was little possibility of 'acquiring' them, especially as I had the luxury of two guards, who never seemed to take their eyes off me.

Two days seemed a reasonable period to sharpen and set the saws, so on the first day I did not do anything controversial. On the second day, I mimed that the file was getting beyond further use: could I search the shed to see if I could find another one? Definitely not! There was no mistaking the answer, which had probably been given earlier by higher authority. Anyway, I persevered, and after much arm waving and miming, one guard searched the various drawers and boxes under my supervision: the other one kept me under close scrutiny to ensure there was no sleight of hand.

It was a bit of a dead loss as the only piece of contraband which I managed to acquire was a four-inch nail: it was equally gratifying to get it through the thorough search in the guardroom. My colleagues were most appreciative of the sharpened saws which gave us even more free time out in the woods.

The wood-cutting parties turned out to be quite rewarding. Although we lost our first contact man with the slave labour girls – they had disappeared when we returned a few days later – the local black market quickly cottoned on to us. The main drawback was the desirability of eating anything we acquired out in the woods, rather than risk taking it back to the Oflag where a snap search would reveal the lax security of our guards. Consequently, we usually enjoyed a relatively substantial lunch before returning home, where our voluntary efforts to keep everyone warm were rewarded with an extra-special meal.

There was one episode which cost me a loss of face. As we became more expert in tree-felling, we found ourselves having more time to spare, so we organised 'big-game' hunting expeditions. The target was wild pig which, we were assured, lived all over the woods around us. Stout poles, sharpened to a point and hardened in the fire, provided spears for the hunters, whilst the remainder of the party acted as beaters. We never saw hide or hair of those fictitious 'ham on the hoof' beasts until I took my turn as a hunter. Excited shouts in the distance told me that our luck had changed.

We had been torturing ourselves with which part of a pig was our individual choice – I recall that pork crackling was my first preference. There were three spearmen on this occasion, with me in the centre, waiting with mouths watering, for the kill!

Never having seen a picture of a wild boar, I had assumed that it would be something like our domestic pig: an easy target which the first thrust should easily reduce to a piece of potential pork crackling. Instead, I was suddenly confronted by an evil grey beast with tusks like the devil's horns and beady red eyes, an apparition that must have come straight from hell. I do not know why it was running away from the beaters, unless it had decided that I was today's dinner. It just did not know what fear was, presumably because I had the local monopoly of the commodity.

The stupid beast could easily have diverted to pass between me and my flanking spearman but, instead it charged straight for me, down the centre of the path, which up to now had seemed an ideal strategic location. If I had known beforehand what a wild boar looked like, there was a faint possibility that I would have stood my ground and tried to let it impale itself on my spear – spare my blushes and at least let me think that I might have done this! As it was, the sight of it completely unnerved me. There was a low branch above me on which I had been sitting, and at the last split second, I hurled my spear straight at its throat and jumped to safety on the branch. The spear just bounced off and the 'devil's disciple' charged straight under my feet and out of sight.

I was subjected to sustained teasing for a long time afterwards. However, we never heard or saw another boar: I was relegated to the role of beater before we abandoned hope of ever getting roast pork on the menu.

Many of our fellow 'kriegies' had been captured prior to the formation of REME and, in their eyes, the Corps had a mystical and divine power over all things electrical and mechanical. It did not take long for the escape committee to co-opt me into their team, with very mixed feelings on my part.

They started their 'sales talk' with a proud display of their toolkit; my heart sank as I knew their primitive nature would dilute the skills in my fingers. Although I had been fortunate enough to serve a first-class apprenticeship in fitting, and felt supremely effective in that role, this confidence was based on the tools which were at my disposal. Without any ambiguity whatsoever, the unskilled labour force which had successfully adapted themselves to these primitive tools over many years, were far more skilled than I could ever hope to be in the short term. Honesty being the best policy, I conveyed my thoughts to the escape committee, but at the same time, offered my services for special duties outside the scope of self-trained technicians.

There was an immediate response: what did I know about skeleton keys? Fortunately, a period in the lock and key section had been part of my apprenticeship training. They had a rusty old door key which had been unearthed some time ago which did not fit any door in our part of the building. Could it be turned

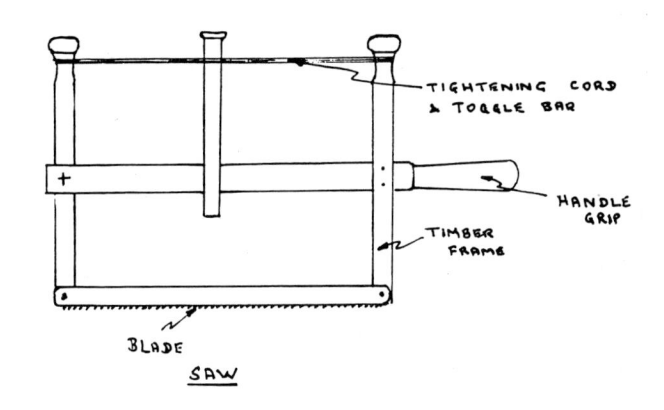

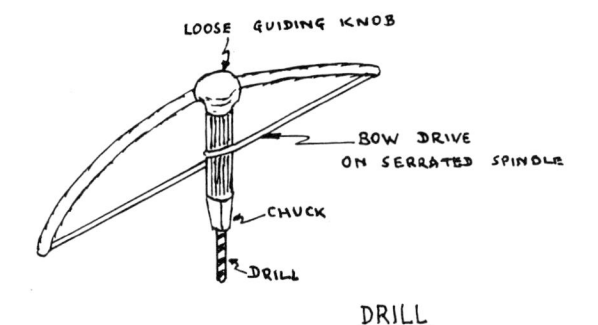

Saw — tightening cord & toggle bar, handle grip, timber frame, blade

Drill — loose guiding knob, bow drive on serrated spindle, chuck, drill

Homemade POW tools

into anything useful? It was a relatively simple job to convert it into a skeleton key which was able to lock and unlock a large number of doors in our part of the building. This rather useless gimmick did substantially increase the esteem for REME.

Another locked basement door was drawn to my attention. It was never used by the Germans, although it was in the boundary line. It was fitted with a rather superior lever lock and had resisted all early efforts. I spent a lot of time manufacturing lock picks from the limited tools and materials available. Normally, it was my nature to evaluate carefully all subsequent possibilities and corrective steps before initiating any action, but this time, metaphorically speaking, I was caught with my pants down!

During the first few attempts I had the services of our standard security guard system, but in view of my lack of success, I asked for it to be disbanded. As soon as I was on my own the lock picking efforts resumed in private. Sod's law then operated and, on the second lone attempt, there was a click and, when I turned the handle, the door opened. It was dark inside but the light from my room showed that it was a short corridor and not another room. I closed the door but all my efforts to lock it proved abortive.

Luck seemed to be against me: when I rushed upstairs to the escape section room they were all missing except for one man who was working on a wooden contraption with the standard 'goon-up' guard system. I had just made up my mind to forget the door and let the Germans have the worry of it at some future date, when I saw a nice screwdriver lying on the table. Brushing aside all his protests, I commandeered the worker, his screwdriver and the 'guard', and took them to the cellar. A careful check indicated it was in the same state as when I left it, so leaving the guard and screwdriver, we explored the short cellar corridor. It seemed to link our door with two more on the opposite side. Whatever was behind these doors was in complete darkness.

We established a security system before stripping the lock out of the door and opening it up. By now my heart was pounding so loudly that I could not understand why the Germans could not hear it. My fingers worked in unison with my heart. Feverishly I slipped the wards out and doctored them to make the lever locks inoperative. After reassembling the lock and fixing it back in position, I was about to close the door when my colleague asked if I had finished. This seemed a particularly stupid question, but I then realised what I had forgotten: he rubbed dirt into the clean screw head slots, and the lock/door joints, to conceal the fact that it had been tampered with. The door locked at the first attempt.

We beat an orderly retreat. The other two resumed their previous work, whilst I took a brisk walk round the yard, taking in deep breaths to try and restore my nervous system. The reprimand for doing this job outside the available security system was accepted without defence on my part; it was fully justified. This, together with the apparent negative results of my efforts left me rather cool about security work for a short time – a period which coincided with the log-cutting activities, so there was plenty to occupy myself.

The Germans obviously knew that we had an illicit radio receiver because they kept holding snap searches to try and find where it was hidden. These were unsuccessful, so they adopted the tactic of severing our electricity supplies during BBC news bulletins. Together with others, I was summoned to a meeting to discuss the possibility of making our own generator. I could not conceal my cynicism when a large electric fan motor was produced and the suggestion made that it could be converted into a generator.

They listened patiently whilst I outlined my limitations in electrical design and the impossibility of manufacturing the conversion parts, etc. When they asked if it was possible for the armature to be shaped with the tools at our disposal I fell straight into the trap. 'That is the easiest part', I replied, not wanting any doubts cast on my skill as a craftsman. I did not have a leg to stand on: it was obvious that they had assessed my potential because a group of university trained boffins had already designed the generator from their available materials, but no one would accept responsibility for the mechanical conversation of the armature – thus, call in the REME. They were really wrong, as I could have selected at least two of the amateur technicians who had developed the skills to do the work involved. They just lacked confidence, which left me holding the baby.

There was a large attic room, normally occupied by our painter colleagues, which was ideal for carrying out this work. A timber window sill had been doctored for a previous job. It lifted out, and, when turned over, had a crude wooden vice in position, available for use. If disturbed, all one had to do was reverse the sill, which automatically tipped the refuse created into the wall cavity and a painter standing by put his paints on top. He then continued his half-finished painting of the view through the window.

The only problem was the armature; being wiser after the

event, we could have secured it separately by string to the vice. As it was, my orders were that if confiscation seemed inevitable, I was to throw it down the cavity. Nobody gave any serious consideration to the possibility of a snap search party beating our security-guard system.

It was a boring job. This helped to focus my brain and it was not long before an alternative solution presented itself. The Germans had segregated their electricity from ours because their lights remained on when ours were off. If, therefore, we could tap into their supply, there would be no need for a generator – what was behind that locked adjoining door?

After an enthusiastic reception a small group of us made a detailed search of the corridor. The obvious solution to plug into the overhead light bulb socket proved disappointing because that circuit was dead, even when our electricity was on. A suggestion that I pick the lock on one of the other doors did not receive an enthusiastic response from me. Instead, I suggested that we try tapping into some electric cables which ran across one end of the corridor before disappearing into the German quarters.

It was agreed to try out this suggestion, but I was politely but firmly guided back to the armature, whilst someone else made the 'tap-in' equipment to my specification. My assistant and I tried it out on a dummy-run; I unlocked the door and we both crept into the corridor. He was holding an oil lamp in one hand and shielding the flame with the other, which left me to carry his electrical 'tap-in'. I thought that he would want to do the 'tap-in' but I was wrong, so once again, I silently cursed the first 'E' of my Corps.

The cable sheath was much tougher than had been anticipated and it took much effort (and multiple prayers) to break through to the bare wire. Everything had appeared to be inert and it came as a great shock when an indicator bulb lit up. In the confined space it seemed like a searchlight and we hastily evacuated to safety. Despondency set in when someone asked the simple question: 'How do you know it is not part of our own system?'

Our enthusiasm was a little dampened when, a few hours later, we huddled in the corridor waiting for our lights to go out, with our now blackened bulb and its elaborate linking network to the radio somewhere high above us – it stayed on! On this occasion I did not suffer the nervous tension which came over me on the first occasion, but the unexpected success nearly had me whooping with joy. The tension, mental and physical, from holding an electrical connection constantly for the next twenty minutes or so, quickly destroyed my ardour.

We repeated this exercise on the next two days, after which our tame 'stool-pigeon' reported the news to the Germans to convince them that we had our own generator. They swallowed this, hook, line and sinker and switched off our electricity which must have inconvenienced them somewhere along the line because the power cut-offs ceased and my blood pressure returned to normal. I was then led gently but firmly back to the armature. Little did I realise my trials and tribulations were far from over.

The great day came when the armature was finished. The last operation had been to remove all 'rags' with a minute file, not much bigger than a nail file, and a small piece of what had once been emery paper. Having satisfied myself with the finished article, I asked the 'stooge' painter to double check its accuracy with the gauge, before taking it downstairs to the eagle-eyed escape committee. Whilst he was doing this I restored the sill to normal and put the tools in my pocket. The painter handed it back to me and confirmed its accuracy, after which we continued to chat. It had been a strain for both of us which tended to build rapport and there did not appear to be any necessity for a hasty divorce.

This was nearly my undoing because, suddenly, there were alarm calls on the landing and stairs. Instinctively, I thrust the armature inside my battledress blouse and rushed towards the door. It was hopeless, so a split second before the German search party crashed in I stopped next to the painter nearest to the door.

The German security sergeant told us to stay where we were before detailing his men to search the room, leaving just one man to guard the door. Apart from myself, there was only the window 'guard' painter in the security team, but the others knew what we had been doing and started 'goon-baiting' to draw attention away from me, the only non-painter in the room. Then the painter next to me started to harangue me about my colour-blindness, his preliminary wink tipped me off as to my response. I vehemently criticised his colouring and the argument raged until I asked the sergeant standing next to me to intervene and adjudicate between us. He was not to be diverted from his duties and I got a very brusque response. There was accumulated years of junk in the attic and his concentration was on the search, not the two idiots standing next to him arguing about colours.

The search proceeded too fast for comfort. As far as I was aware, there was nothing for them to find of a security nature apart from my appendages, but it could be followed by a body search, and even a blind man could not have missed an armature. After some further wrangling with the painter, I asked *sotto voce*, because we had been told to keep quiet, permission to go to the urinal; I received a very firm negative reply. I then demanded an escort to the urinal and, again, a firm negative. I replied that I was not going to wet my trousers for him, or Hitler, and my guardian angel intervened once more. One of the guards found something interesting in a box and the sergeant moved away from me towards it. I turned to the guard at the door and waved him to follow me as I stepped into the corridor. He hesitated a split second too long, before calling out to the sergeant. By the time he received his orders it was too late: I had disappeared round the corner into the crowd of onlookers.

It was a scene reminiscent of the 'Keystone Cops' as we tore down the stairs; the guard was close behind me but, of course, had more difficulty getting through the crowd. The armature was slung to one of the many pairs of waiting hands, with a skill usually reserved for the All Blacks rugby team. The tools in my pocket were far more difficult to extract on the gallop, and I only managed to pass them just outside the toilet.

The guard burst into the toilet a few seconds after me, closely followed by the sergeant, to find me urinating with extravagant sounds of relief and pleasure. What followed was not unexpected, but the temporary physical discomfort was alleviated by my knowledge of having outwitted them, and the fact that they could search me, my bunk and belongings, without finding anything of a controversial nature.

The German security officer conducting the final interview was not one of our favourite pin-ups, and things did not bode well for me. Attack being the best form of defence, I adopted an attitude of affronted dignity, claiming that the Geneva Convention did not authorise them to make me wet my trousers. This did not make much impression until I accidentally laid the blame on the sergeant for not acceding to my request for an escort to take me to the urinal.

The sergeant did not appear to have included this fact in his report. He was probably more concerned about covering his own back as to how I had escaped from under his guard. To my astonishment, this item seemed to be conclusive proof of my innocence, in the eyes of my interrogator. You could have knocked me down with a feather. After the officer had received confirmation of this fact from the sergeant, he reprimanded me for my stupidity, which could have had tragic consequences. He pointed out that the rough treatment which I had received was entirely my own fault and let me go free!

After this episode, I lay low on any security work. The only other undercover work I did was to balance the flywheel drive to the generator. I did not know whether or not it was ever assembled, because we evacuated the Oflag shortly afterwards.

Normally, the war seemed a long way away. We only had one exciting incident in mid-December, when our fighter planes shot-up a train close to the camp, to the great excitement of the older prisoners who stood cheering at the windows. The newer prisoners did not share their confidence that the guards in the towers would not open fire on them. We turned out to be right, although to be fair to the Germans, when they hit the wall to the side of one of the windows, it must have been deliberately aimed there, because the range was less than one hundred yards.

As winter hardened its grip, snow was built up into an embankment in the yard and the area inside was flooded with water, which we had to pay for, and there was a wonderful skating rink. The Canadians abandoned their incessant poker schools and produced genuine Canadian ice hockey skates. I quickly found out everyone who owned my size and borrowed from them at every opportunity as soon as they left the ice. I gained confidence through watching the experts and quickly adapted to this new sport, even trying my hand at ice hockey, until a rather violent bodycheck made me realise I was playing with fire. After this I contented myself with simple circuits.

Several pairs of skis were produced when we went on parole walks, but I could not master this technique: I soon abandoned the effort to concentrate instead on collecting all things edible.

The nights tended to drag a little because, to conserve electricity, the Germans changed all bulbs to 25 watts. This left even the poker players squinting at their cards, and reading in artificial light was impossible. The padre's insistence on writing home when we arrived at the Oflag bore fruit on 3 February, when I received my first letter from my fiancée dated 8 December. She had received the first one from me on the same day. I did not receive the one written by my mother on the same day, until five weeks later.

Around mid-March, we had a new intake of prisoners who had been evacuated from their camp in the east, and marched westward from the advancing Russians. One of them, a padre, gave some fascinating talks on how to survive the rigours and hardships of such a forced march. I was an avid listener, and the information he imparted was to have a profound effect on my well-being in the near future.

Little by little the signs of war grew closer; flights of American bombers overhead – occasionally we could see one in trouble. Air raid warnings became frequent and inconvenient: we had to retire indoors and thus, miss the early spring sunshine, but the order to evacuate the Oflag came very unexpectedly and caught a lot of people out. I was prepared for it and had sorted out and packed my emergency pack, based on the lectures given by the padre. Like a true optimist, the day before we left I planted cucumber seeds in the garden. It was quieter in the little conservatory; the bedrooms were a mass of heaving bodies trying to decide what to take with them. Some of the longer serving prisoners had collected quite a substantial wardrobe over the years.

I felt sorry for people like the painters, many of whom left behind four years' work. We were told that all possessions left in the Oflag would be returned to their owners in due course – they never were; anyone who believed that statement really wanted his head examined. All the same, I would criticise our senior British officers for making the statement in the first place. No doubt it was done with the best of intentions so that people did not overload themselves for the march, but, in the long run, I bet it broke a lot of hearts.

CHAPTER 6

The March to Freedom

DAY 1: **In the fresh air to Rückenßuss**

Reveille was at 6a.m. on 29 March 1945, early enough for a 12 noon projected start time, which, in the event, was postponed until 2.20p.m. I attended the last Holy Communion at the Oflag: it got me away from the bedlam in the living quarters. It was announced that the Germans were going to provide us with a lorry to carry heavy kit. I only handed in my bedroll, as I did not intend to be parted from the emergency pack which had been prepared to cover most emergencies.

Somehow the lorry got lost on the first day's march; I was thankful that I had not parted with my kit. The lorry turned up in the night, but in the meantime, there had been a lot of panic.

During the march I was able to indulge in stealing milk from the churns standing at the side of the road awaiting collection. When a batch hove into sight it was relatively easy to detach my enamel mug off its home-made hook on the haversack, lift the churn lid with my left hand whilst quickly, but carefully, scooping the cream off the top of the milk – with the connivance of friendly guards looking the other way and smoking my cigarettes. Our overnight billet on the first night was a large barn, rather crowded, but with electric light.

I did well for food on that first night because of retaining my pack. In addition, even though it was nearly midnight, the black market was 'open' and I was able to supplement supper with what my diary refers to as 'sour milk', more commonly known nowadays as yoghurt: in those days it was rare in the UK. All in all, it was rather pleasant: the mental intoxication of being outside prison walls, the pleasure of wandering through some beautiful open countryside in the early spring weather, the relaxed physical fatigue from the unaccustomed exercise. This, coupled with the excitement of milk pilferage and the boundless possibilities of future black market opportunities left me feeling happy and relaxed.

The majority of my colleagues were not in such a happy frame of mind, as most of their possessions were on the missing lorry. I did make a comment to one of my friends about the 'wise and foolish virgins' in the bible, but his response was not in accordance with the good book, in fact the words he used were not even in it. I nestled down in the loose straw, ensured all my belongings were safely stowed away, before drifting off into a deep relaxing sleep.

DAY 2: To Hoheneiche – RAF Activity

In view of the restricted toilet facilities, I got up early next morning to enjoy them on a leisurely basis, and then went out looking for a black market. I did so well, that I knew I would not be able to carry it all, so my close friends and I literally stuffed ourselves with a huge omelette for breakfast, before loading what we could not carry on to the lorry which, as already mentioned, turned up during the night. My emergency rations for the day were two hard-boiled eggs and a bottle of yoghurt milk.

We did not leave until 11.30a.m. The day started well, as the roads were good for marching even though my pack was rather heavy with black market goodies. I left my overcoat on the lorry with the bedroll so that body movement was not so restricted. After stopping for lunch at Sontra, we ran into aerial activity. The first time the RAF Typhoons dived towards us, there was a flash of red berets as the 'airborne' hit the ditch at the side of the road – to the derision of the older prisoners, who had a childlike faith in the large PW recognition signs which we pegged out in the hope that Allied planes would not mistake us for a German column.

A short time later, whilst the banter was still going on, another

The forced march (1–16 = overnight stays)

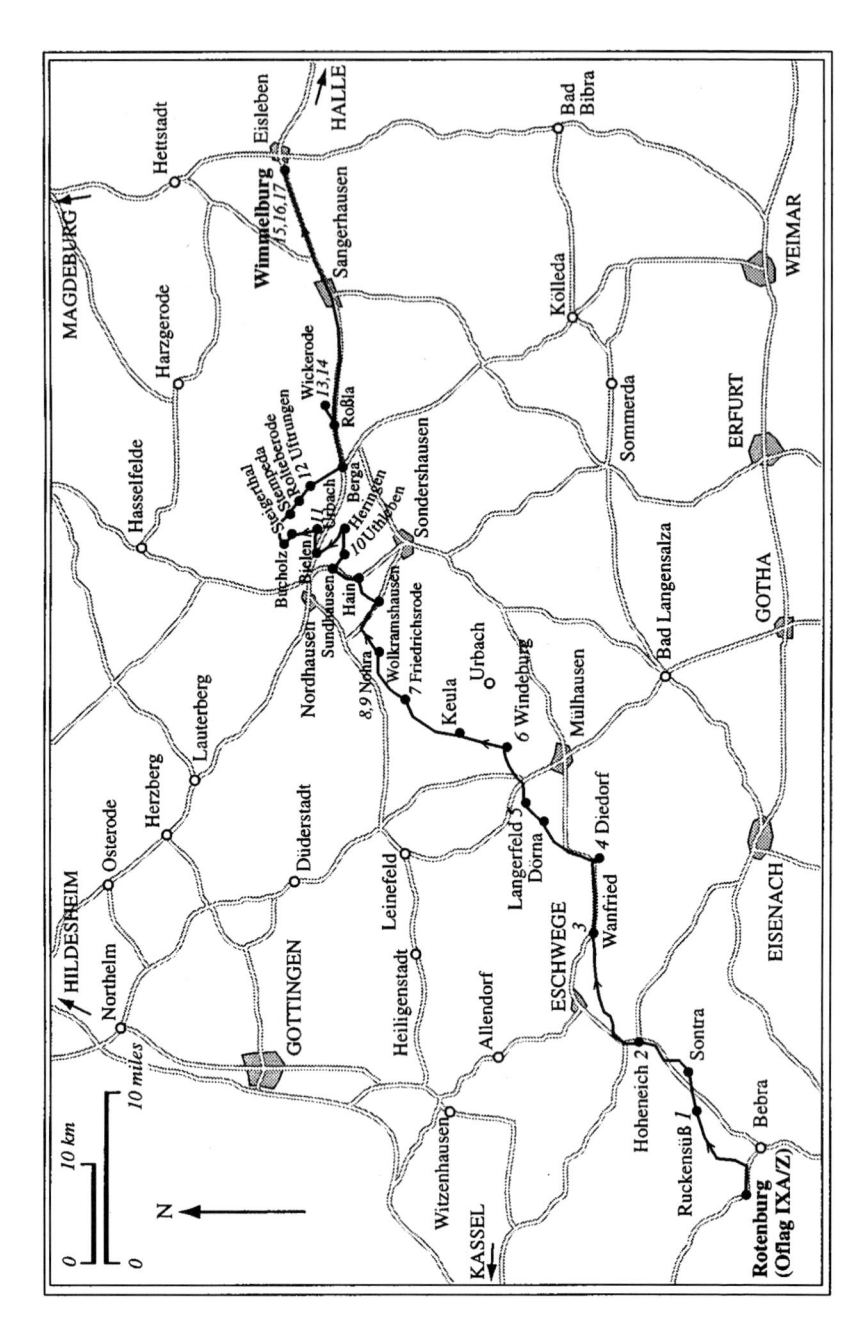

formation of Typhoons came into view as we were passing a railway marshalling yard. This time they came down in an attack formation and blasted a train about fifty yards to our right: the 'Red Devils' were already in the ditch when they were flattened by the mass of bodies jumping on top of them. There was no more banter: they got the message when they saw the remnants of the train, after the RAF's 'tin openers' had been at work.

For some unknown reason, we had to collect our bedrolls off the lorry after lunch and carry them which caught out a lot of people. Some of them had no alternative but to jettison some of their possessions; I just managed to cope with my load, but I was glad that it was not any heavier. To add to the mystery, we were given a lift on the lorry for the last mile or so to our night billet, in a large barn at Hoheneiche. The air raids had eliminated all the electric lights so we had to spend a miserable cold night: we could not open our bedrolls for fear of losing valuable possessions in the loose straw.

On the first day we covered 19km, in nearly 9½ hours, and on the second day we marched 17km.

DAY 3: Milk sickness – Wanfried

I woke up just after 6a.m. on the third day feeling really sick, so sick, in fact that I could not face any breakfast – which says it all really. At that time I thought it must be due to something I had eaten; in retrospect, I realise that it was probably the milk which had created the problem. Milk has always been one of my favourite drinks, and over the last two days I must have drunk nearly a gallon. What nobody appreciated in those days was that milk in the stomach encourages any bugs there to breed; it was commonly thought that milk was an invalid food, therefore, the sicker I felt, the more milk I drank to build up my strength and thereby accentuated the problem.

On the morning of 31 March 1945, there was tremendous air activity and shelling all round us. The Germans actually considered moving us to some woods about 4km away and waiting there for the attacking Americans to relieve us. In the end, our senior British officer agreed with the German Commandant that he would give parole on our behalf not to escape and we would keep moving.

I still do not understand why parole should have been given at that stage but, at the time, I felt so ill I could not get interested in what was going on around me. The morning was a bit of a nightmare, the marching pace was forced, with no reasonable rest periods allowed. After starting at 10.30a.m. the first real break did not come until 4pm, by which time I was virtually all-in with a severe bout of diarrhoea. A mug of tea and some dry bread, coupled with more RAF attacks at Eschwege, restored me a little. The attacks were conventional close support air sorties, so we knew that our ground forces were very close behind us. Later on, I staggered into our overnight billet, in a farm 2km beyond Wanfried: no straw in the barn, just bare boards, but we were not caught out this time and 'fat' lamps were soon spluttering into life. I slept in my bedroll for the first time, and had a long satisfying sleep after a lengthy sojourn in the 'bogs', where I managed to get rid of what had been upsetting my tummy. Our well-earned night's rest was somewhat disturbed by the sound of German reinforcements, rushing past us to defend against the Allied bridgehead.

DAY 4: **A short march – Diedort**

April Fools Day dawned bright and early for me at 6.30a.m. to discover I felt a lot fitter, although my tummy still felt unsettled. I handed in tea, eggs and porridge towards a communal breakfast, which I managed to keep down. After this I went off to celebrate Holy Communion. After the mad rush of yesterday, things appeared more stable; presumably, the German reinforcements were holding the line somewhere in our rear. We had seen some shot-up transports near a troop of Indo-Frenchmen and it was obvious that the roads in this area were a bit unhealthy.

We did not set off until 1p.m., and only marched 7km to Diedorf, where the parole mystery was solved. The German guards were stationed facing outwards, leaving us to walk freely in a designated area. We were billeted in small groups in a residential area, mostly in small barns. Mugs of tea were issued at 5.45p.m., followed by bacon and potatoes at 6.30p.m. There was no electric light in the room above the stables, where I was sleeping, but I managed to wash and shave before retiring in anticipation of an early start the following morning. The only disturbance that night came from the horses in the barn beneath us. They did not seem to sleep in the conventional meaning of the word.

DAY 5: **Easy walk to Lengefeld**

The clocks altered during the night, so we were up bright and early, just after 6a.m. We had breakfast at 7.30a.m. of tea, bacon and bread, supplemented with communal porridge made from a large bucketful of crushed oats, which I had traded for a bar of soap. It tasted a bit yucky, but it did at least fill us up, as there was more than enough for anyone who fancied it. The march started earlier than usual, at 9a.m. We did 11km before stopping at Dörna for lunch. It was an easy day which belied the early start, because we only marched a further 2km before arriving at our overnight billet at Lengefeld.

We arrived at Lengefeld relatively early, around 3.45p.m., which was to our advantage, because we were in a barn in the middle of a very large muddy field, with no water supply. We had plenty to occupy ourselves with in the remaining daylight hours. In spite of the restrictions I managed to acquire some black market bread off a boy, before retiring for a good night's sleep, after a cooked supper including bacon.

DAY 6: **A good billet at Windeberg**

Our sixth day on the march started with reveille at 7.15a.m. and a mug of tea at 7.30a.m. We left Lengefeld at 10.05a.m. and took the Dingelstadt road for 2km, before turning right towards

Mülhausen which was still only 10km away. The billet that night at Windeberg turned out to be the best to date, with very friendly inhabitants. Rumours that our troops were near Mülhausen, seemed to be substantiated when German troops evacuated their wounded from the little cottage hospital, before moving out themselves. The villagers and ourselves then raided the bakery.

Revised parole regulations were now implemented; this gave us official authority to trade, but in return, lights out was at 8.30p.m. Having acquired plenty of bread in the raid on the bakery, I changed my diet by making a bread pudding, flavoured with cocoa powder and apricots from my emergency ration pack, which I had decided to lighten. This was followed by three helpings of official soup which, for a change, was in abundance, as most people were enjoying the freshly baked bread.

DAY 7: Blackmarketing – Friedrichsrode

We were getting more organised in our personal routines. The diary records that on the next morning, having stayed in bed until 7.15a.m., I managed to complete my toilet functions, then fry up some bread for Reggie and I in the house where we had been billeted, drink 1½ pints of milk, and get my bottle filled before a 9.0a.m. departure.

I cannot recall when I first gained access to the villagers' homes; it could have been in this village, because fried bread indicates a frying pan and fat, which I certainly did not possess. As a generalisation, we found the Harz mountain people a friendly bunch; it was very rare to come across a dedicated Nazi. Elderly ladies and young children were the best to negotiate with on the black market, because the age groups in between were either away fighting or scared of being caught trading. The old ladies did not care a damn, and if you asked them to cook the food which you had just bartered off them, they did so readily: I never got a refusal.

Although we had only just got official permission to fraternise with the locals, I and a few others had been doing it since we left the Oflag. In the first instance I used guidance from the friendly guards whom I had been cultivating over the past few months, but I was probably the first to realise the potential of young children. Boys will be boys and the Germans are no exception, so long as they had not been contaminated by the Hitler Youth Movement. It was a great challenge to young boys to sneak past our guards and exchange vegetables, which were in abundant supply, for cigarettes in particular. I can visualise their triumphant return to friends and family carrying their trophies. If you asked them for something else such as onions, they would rush away to circumvent another guard further round the perimeter, having made themselves obvious to the ones in our sector, with cheeky repartee as they rushed out past them.

Little girls were the best at this novel game, usually two of them, hand in hand, with the elder holding a small basket in one hand and her younger accomplice with the other. Unlike the boys, who openly solicited for trade, the little girls just stood there with their big eyes gazing at the novel sights around them, ignored by the guards and the majority of the POWs. Show them a bar of soap or a few cigarettes, however, and they became far more efficient traders than their brothers.

I recall one incident when my padre friend and I were trying to communicate with two little girls, one about eight or nine years old and the other just a little toddler. They had drifted into our lines during an early phase, when the guards were trying to keep the boys out. The padre gave them a bar of soap – they did not have anything to trade and were only there out of curiosity: his gift was of a charitable nature, not a trading one. Some time later, the same little girls came back into our lines carrying a basket. The guard just smiled benevolently at them as they passed right under his nose, before bending down to pick up a stone to throw at a boy who was trying to dodge in with them.

The girls walked straight up to the padre and removed the cloth covering the basket to reveal its contents: hot steaming boiled potatoes in their jackets, straight from the pan. He was most embarrassed, so we told him that he had no option but to accept the return gift, as otherwise, the girls would feel rejected. They tasted delicious. With great dignity the two little girls waved bye-bye to all of us, walked straight up to the nearest guard and said bye-bye to him before walking away, again straight under his nose.

There did not seem to be any great food shortage in these mountain villages, so it was no great hardship on their part to exchange it for soap and cigarettes, which they craved for. The best combination in the latter stages, when we were billeted in close proximity to the village houses, was to find girls who would take you to their grandmother. After the all-male company in the Oflag, it was unbelievably civilised to sit around a kitchen table, eating a bartered meal which grandmother had just cooked for you, whilst she fussed around her new found temporary family.

The atmosphere, whenever I was lucky enough to experience it, was always the same. The children would try to improve their limited English vocabulary by holding items up, whilst I repeated the appropriate word; grandmother would bustle around like a mother hen and take a great interest in my family photographs, but if mother popped in, she would soon disappear again, presumably out of fear of any subsequent reprisals from Nazis.

I was fortunate enough always to have an abundant supply of black market goodies because, apart from what I had saved up, I received like everyone else, a generous last minute distribution before we left the Oflag. Then, on the day we had been told to remove our bedrolls from the lorry and carry them, many people had jettisoned their soap stocks on account of the weight. Preference, of course, was given to holding on to their cigarettes. At that time I was heavily weighted down and not feeling well, but I could not leave all that soap lying in the grass, so I joined a few more far-seeing souls and collected it up. Soap was undoubtedly the best trading item in the Harz mountains. As it turned out, we only had to carry our bedrolls for the one afternoon and, after that, my heavy soap stocks were carried on the lorry each day, in my bedroll. I was the equivalent of a soap millionaire at a time and place where it was in strong demand.

Another quirk of memory: although our own Oflag transport

played such a vital part in our lives at that stage, I cannot remember what it looked like. On the other hand, a reminder from my diary brought back a vivid recollection of one motorised convoy which passed us. No vehicle ever appeared to travel singly; it would always be towing two or three other vehicles or trailers, obviously to conserve fuel. The funniest we saw was a truck, piled high with furniture, towing a trailer full of cattle, and behind that, three more loaded trucks, all as big as the towing truck. At the rear of this convoy was a very large expensive saloon car, complete with a very dignified family and piled-up luggage. I do not know what the Germans used in their clutch plates, but they were obviously light-years ahead of the British.

We often saw vehicles loaded to overflowing with women and children, and in most cases with spotters sitting on the bonnet to give warning of attacking aircraft. These vehicles were a legitimate target for Allied aircraft; unlike us, they were not to know that they were carrying women and children. There was no possibility of their being able to evacuate the lorries in the event of an air attack. I have often wondered if the women realised what danger they were putting themselves in, they would have been much safer pushing a pram.

Having strayed somewhat from the sequence in my dairy, I am now going back to the seventh day of our march, Wednesday 4 April 1945. As noted earlier, we set off around 9a.m. in bright weather conditions. The route was mainly uphill in wooded country, and after approximately 7km, we arrived at Keula around noon and lunch was taken. The weather changed for the worse: hailstones and a bitter wind in an exposed position somewhat dampened our ardour, but after my earlier illness, my strength was returning and I felt much better.

The gunfire sounded quite close and planes still appeared to be shooting targets in the vicinity of Mülhausen: by now, these battle noises were quite commonplace and we hardly noticed them. After lunch, we continued through the same type of countryside, until we arrived at Friedrichsrode about 3.30p.m. We were billeted here overnight. I set off looking for a black market with another chap, but the place seemed absolutely dead. All we managed to acquire was some potatoes and onions which we fried up to supplement the meal we had to supply from our own packs: no meal was forthcoming from the cookhouse. Reggie and I did not fare too badly, dining off potatoes and onion with three slices of bread and half an egg each, followed by bread pudding as dessert. After a hot drink, I retired to bed early, but spent an uncomfortable night as a late arrival lay across my foot space and I could not stretch out my feet. How he slept through my kicks is beyond my comprehension. I heard him complaining next morning saying that he must have slept on something hard because his ribs ached! I felt sorry for his wife or wife to be, because he just 'died' in bed.

DAY 8: **Nohra**

In trouble again next morning as I had to dash out of bed early to the bogs: the 'squitters' all over again, damn it! There was no point in going back to bed, so I washed and shaved before toasting seven slices of bread to try and settle my tummy. Fortunately, I did not have the nausea of the previous attack, and I was glad to leave this poor billet and step out in good heart about 10a.m.

Again, our route was predominantly cross-country, through very pleasant woods. We stopped for lunch in a little village in the valley below the woods. I am guessing, because my diary does not mention a particular air-raid which we observed when passing through country like this, but it could well be the day when it happened. We were walking on a track following the contour lines on hills overlooking the junction of two valleys, in the centre of which was a small town: it was not very big but it was not possible to guess the number of inhabitants because everything happened so quickly.

Our personal concern was Allied fighter planes. We did not take too much notice of the heavy bombers flying overhead; we were not the type of target they were normally after. When the large formation of heavy bombers came into view over our left shoulder our only thought was that they were flying lower than normal – we soon found out why. Suddenly, there was the whine of falling bombs. I looked across and had a brief sight of what appeared to be a sleepy little town, similar to many we had passed through, before it disappeared into a haze of dust and flames. Whatever the Allies thought was in the town was completely obliterated, because wave after wave of bombers followed the first one. All they did was drop their bombs in the heart of the dust cloud which was being carried high into the sky with the heat of the flames.

There was no cheering from our column, and a deathly silence fell on us for the next hour or so. It is one thing to kill men, that is what we were trained to do, but to massacre women and children on that scale reduced our credibility to the same level as the Nazis in the concentration camps. We were not proud to be on the same side as the man who had authorised that raid. There were no German fighters to defend it, and not a solitary anti-aircraft gun opened fire; it was all rather obscene.

On second thoughts, this raid must have occurred much later on because we received a very friendly reception at our next overnight billet. Generally speaking we were lucky that 'strategic bombing', as the planners called it, took place after we had passed through a town. Had it been otherwise it might well have been unfortunate for us. It is well recorded that many of our airmen suffered at the hands of mobs after they had parachuted to safety from crashing planes. Historians may criticise such episodes in retrospect, but they do not know what they are talking about. If I had been wearing a grey uniform I might have done the same.

On that eighth day on the march, we arrived at our destination reasonably early at 3.15p.m. I found myself billeted in a large barn at Nohra, with 'C' company. I made myself some porridge for supper followed by a section meal of potatoes and meat paste. All the farms in the villages were manned by slave labourers under the supervision of their German owners: all able-bodied men were in the forces. The slave labour force was drawn from all over Europe: every nationality seemed to be represented in some form or other. Their physical well-being varied considerably, according to the luck of the draw. For example girls, who seemed to be in the majority, looked reasonably well looked after if they were fortunate enough to be posted to a particular farm. No farmer ill treats his stock otherwise it affects his yield and so the wise ones looked upon the girls in the same light.

We had quite an amusing episode whilst billeted at Nohra, when a little Polish girl about four or five years old, decided to entertain us. She started by singing what sounded like a nursery rhyme. Following our enthusiastic applause she broke into a dance. One of the musically gifted men in our group produced a recorder, whilst others tried to instruct us in an appropriate beat. The result was quite good, and the little girl, flushed with success, danced enthusiastically; our 'conductors' kept us humming and clapping in rhythm and the mother appeared to prompt her child – a very good time was had by all.

After the 'show' several people went round with the hat and everyone gave generously; the mother was taken aback by the large number of gifts her daughter received. I think this was spontaneous, since our arrival in that part of the country was something new. They might have tried it out on German troops passing through the village who would, undoubtedly, have enjoyed the show as much as we did. If so, it showed enterprise.

The black market was quite good – five eggs, some flour and potatoes rewarded my efforts. On my return to the billet I found that my overcoat had disappeared so that the night was cold and miserable. Furthermore, I had squitters during the night, but things looked up when I found my overcoat next morning, in the far corner of the barn. Someone, who was an officer, but no gentleman, never got another chance to improve his body warmth at the expense of mine.

DAY 9: **Nohra – Escape plans**

Next morning, washed, shaved etc, in anticipation of an early start, only to be told that this was to be a rest-day. Traded for milk off a little girl and got her to introduce me to grandmother, who was actually running the farm. It was relatively easy to get my feet under the kitchen table. I had noticed a large galvanised iron bathtub hanging in the yard and I asked Grandma if I could use it; 'Certainly', she said, so I put a pan of water on the stove to heat it up. It was cold outside but the sun was shining. I found a nice quiet corner, opened an empty stable door outwards to act as a windbreak, and placed the bath in the sun. I half filled the bath with cold water before collecting my pan of boiling water – it only took the chill off the water. Stripped-off, I stood in the bath and thoroughly washed my feet, working up to the calves, thigh and crotch.

I had just reached the stage of lathering my buttocks when a hand grasped my thigh. A voice said something in German, before a big black kettle spout appeared next to my body. A stream of boiling hot water just missed my intimate masculinity and my feet and toes. My immediate reaction was one of frozen fear; I hardly dared move a muscle, but there was no embarrassment when I found that the person Grandma had sent out with a supplementary supply of hot water was a very attractive female teenager. The location of her hand was insignificant compared to the accuracy of her aim.

As soon as she finished pouring, I sat down before thanking her, to the ribald comments of my friends who had seen her approaching with the kettle and anticipated the outcome. There was quite a queue for the bath after I had finished with it, but no one else got the same personal maid service. Nice and clean again, with fresh underclothes on, I negotiated with Grandma for one of the girls to wash the dirty undies and socks which were then dried out over the stove, ready for repacking in my haversack that night. After this, I set out to explore our surroundings. In the meantime, my friends had traded for a handcart to collect wood for their cooking fires; I did it the easy way – Grandma cooked mine!

After lunch, I spread my black market activities a little further, obtaining peas and beans from some Italians, and eggs and cake from a Pole, to take with me next day. I could have obtained these from Grandma, but I enjoyed a fresh challenge. Four of us had a long discussion about our future prospects under the Third Reich. We were all feeling physically much stronger, and had lost the permanent hunger ache of the last few months.

Warnings had been issued that escaping POWs risked being shot out of hand by the Allgemeine SS – the political version of the SS who were used by Himmler to man concentration camps – as opposed to the Waffen SS who were fighting troops. Although we firmly believed this threat, at the same time we were very wary of our future prospects. If we had known about the earlier massacre of Polish officers by their Russian captors, and had been gifted with the ability to look into the future to see the despicable behaviour of one of our own generals in comparable circumstances, we would have been more than worried.

We were quite happy to continue to march in front of our advancing army because we knew that when the opportune moment arose, tanks could quickly overtake our marching column. However, if any effort was made to load us on a train, that would be a different kettle of fish. The other three of our discussion group had been transported to prison in cattle trucks; they were adamant that a break for freedom must be made before we were loaded on to any train. Afterwards, it would be most difficult and every minute of the journey would take us further and further from potential freedom. Arising from our discussions we agreed that (a) the four of us, three Airborne and one Kiwi, would stick together, no more and no less; (b) if we slipped away during the night, we would try to do so complete with bedrolls in addition to haversacks; (c) we would march in the column in a group, so that if it was a daylight break, we would be together; (d) it was undesirable to kill anyone during our escape efforts, as the resultant German search would be on a much larger scale to ensure recapture; (e) we would not try to break through the German lines, instead we would go covert and wait for the battlefield to roll over us; and (f) a proposed train journey would automatically trigger an escape attempt and, in a similar manner, any journey by road transport of more than one hour's duration would do likewise.

The small handcart which we had just purchased held all our kit, so there was no necessity to put anything on the lorry and we were now ready for all contingencies. All in all, it had been a most enjoyable day, spoilt only by the fact that my over-loaded tummy played up again during the night.

DAY 10: **Uthleben**

The tenth day, Saturday 7 April, dawned nice and bright after the poorer weather of the previous evening. I got up early to enjoy a leisurely ablution in the outhouse of the Poles' quarters, they having departed earlier for work. Grandma did me some toast for breakfast and I said my goodbyes before joining the column for the 9.30a.m. start time. We did 3km to Wolkramshausen and a further 1km to Ruxleben, in glorious sunshine, before climbing a hill to Hain, where we had lunch in an orchard. It was a generous 1½hrs lunchbreak before going on to Sundhausen and then turning right to Uthleben 3km further on. (I think it might have been during this journey that we observed the blanket bombing mentioned earlier. My diary notes that the local populace was not very friendly because of bombing in their vicinity.)

We arrived at our billet in Uthleben about 4.15p.m. It turned out to be a meeting hall, with a pub on one side and a butcher's shop on the other. We even had tables and chairs to enjoy our meal of macaroni and cheese in civilised surroundings. The amount issued per person was microscopic, but we quickly supplemented this with our own nutritious black market stew – with two different meats in it, thanks to a Frenchman who became the owner of some genuine pipe tobacco. He, in turn, introduced us to a carpenter who worked most of the night doing repairs to our handcart, again with pipe tobacco as the trading medium. By now, the others were getting low in trading items so 'Rothschild' REME had to handle the necessary trading.

After the earlier disturbed nights, it was a pleasure to sink into a deep relaxing sleep from which I did not wake up until 7.15a.m. Tummy was not entirely at ease, so I restricted myself to just three slices of toast for breakfast.

DAY 11: **Bucholz – An SS incident**

The eleventh day's march started at 9.30a.m. in nice weather. The first 3km were to Heringen, then turning left to Windehausen a further 3km away. As we rested there we watched flight after flight of our heavy bombers trundle across the sky. The next destination was Bielen some 4km away, and another 3km to Urbach, where we had lunch under some trees, next to some German Luftwaffe doing the same thing. Our intended billet at Steigerthal, 5km further along the road, had been bombed before our arrival. It was full of very unfriendly refugees, so the decision was made to carry on a further 4km to Buchbiz.

As we marched down the road there was an incident which could have had tragic consequences. As we marched in columns of three, a captain in the Allgemeine SS suddenly stepped out in front of the right-hand file, which veered to its left to walk round him. After about half the column had done this, a very large Canadian officer kept a straight path until he was forced to stop in front of the SS man. Our little squad was just behind him, so we stopped as well, which brought the whole column to a shuffling halt. For at least a full minute the two of them just stood there, eyeball to eyeball, before the German snarled something which got an equally vicious response from the German-speaking Canadian.

It was an explosive situation, not made any better when one of our senior officers and our German security captain joined in the discussion. The response to do what the SS officer had demanded was a pithy refusal from the Canadian, who seemed hell-bent on committing suicide because the SS man now had a revolver in his hand. All German-speaking officers in the immediate vicinity were offering advice, the most novel one I think, from subsequent descriptions, was 'when you get to hell sort the German bastard out who killed you – he will be the one with his balls stuffed in his mouth' – very succinct!

The British senior officer was having an apoplectic fit; he could not face all of us simultaneously, and no matter which way he turned, voices behind him questioned his 'LMF'[1] and blatantly stripped away his authority: it was open mutiny. The overall docile and resigned atmosphere in the marching column was transformed, within two minutes, into an emotional lynch mob. The guards unslung their rifles but this had no effect and nobody took the slightest notice.

The German Commandant came on the scene, gave a brief command to the SS man, who moved back immediately on to the pavement, and we marched on again. It was over as quickly as it started, but nobody seemed to hear the order which motivated the SS man to get out of the way. I wish I knew what had been said to him, it could not have been more than half a dozen words, but it was very, very effective. It was a localised incident, the majority of the column did not know what had been going on, and I doubt whether they ever realised the repercussions this incident could have had on our lives.

The improvised billet at Buchholz was a large barn with only dirty straw to sleep on: a retrograde step from our deluxe accommodation of the previous nights. I was mystified by the fact that we appeared to be only 7km from Nordhausen, and unable to determine why this was so after all the distance we had covered. For obvious reasons we were not allowed out in the village, but our packs were full of black market food, so we cooked on larger than normal wood fires.

DAY 12: **Uftrungen**

I had another good night's sleep and woke up refreshed just after 6a.m. Porridge, toast and an egg shared with Reggie for breakfast. He was concerned about yesterday's incident with the SS officer.

---

1   Lack of moral fibre.

He was convinced that the officer would come back with troops to exact retribution; he could not understand why we refused to take this seriously. He announced his intention to escape, by himself if necessary, as soon as possible.

We appealed and protested vehemently to no avail; his mind was made up, and nothing we said made any impression on him. I was most upset because he was my particular friend; a really nice man and probably a very good officer, but not 'street-wise' when it came down to covert-style operations. We argued that the Germans were far too committed against the American offensive to merit even the SS officer withdrawing men in order to settle a personal grudge: even if he came back it would only be with a handful of men, and our Camp Commandant had already displayed his command over the situation. In the final analysis, there were too many red berets in our column to encourage these concentration camp-trained cowards to mix it with us – the egoism of the airborne forces cancelled out the fact that they would be armed and we could only put our guards' weapons to better use.

He was still adamant; I had never seen him in this mood before. He admitted to me privately that, having endured four years in a prison camp, he just could not face up to losing his life in the last minute. My diary records that 'I let him have my 1/3rd Commissar for escape purposes'. Forty-five years on, I do not have the faintest recollection of what I meant by that phrase.

I conducted a careful search of our limited movement area and 'found' some potatoes and a small amount of wheat which was loaded on to the lorry for future communal use.

The twelfth day's march started at 9.45a.m., covering 4km to Stempeda and then 2km to Rottleberode, where we had a one hour lunch break surrounded by signs of extensive bomb damage. No tea was available so I contented myself by nibbling a hard-boiled egg. After lunch we only went another 4km to a state farm at Uftrungen, which I noted in my diary as the best to date. I do not remember why I gave it that category, but judging by the fact that my black market activities yielded two bottles of milk, a dozen eggs and German sausages, in addition to beer, lemonade and sausage sandwiches, the rating must, I think, have been strongly influenced by the quantity of food on offer.

The official meal issue was pea soup. The diary records: 'sat in the sun – beautiful – very, very full'. I found a barber's shop which was closed unfortunately, and I could not have a much needed haircut. I clearly recall taking part in a discussion that night, sitting round a large kitchen table with two Germans, three Dutchmen and Reggie: generally putting the world right, whilst eating sandwiches and drinking beer. The others were concentrating on smoking themselves to death. I slept in a passageway which was not the best place to select; the unaccustomed large quantity of food and drink which had been consumed, resulted in a steady flow of POWs to the bogs at the end of the corridor.

DAY 13: **Dittichenrode – Another SS incident**

The thirteenth day of our march dawned brightly at 6.15a.m. when I gave up trying to sleep in 'Piccadilly Circus'. There was such a heavy demand for the bogs that I thought it would be wise to stake an early claim. After attention to nature, I returned to the kitchen when I enjoyed a fried egg on toast with a glass of milk for breakfast.

It was quite hot when we started our day's march at 9.30a.m. Fortunately, we only had to do 6km to Berna, before stopping for an early lunch break at 11.30a.m. I stripped off to the waist to enjoy a bit of sunbathing, whilst heavy Allied bombing echoed all round us. Our one-hour break was extended by half-an-hour because several waves of our fighters started to shoot up the adjacent railway sidings. A combination of very hot weather and heavy air attacks kept us jumping in and out of ditches all afternoon, making us very hot in every sense of the term.

As soon as we got a break in the attacks, we fairly ran away from Berna towards Roßla, which was 4km away. We then carried on to Dittichenrode. Here we had another incident with another SS officer and a POW called Goodall. Again it seemed like deliberate provocation on the part of the SS man but, this time, it was quickly squashed by our German security captain who had obviously been taking lessons from his Commandant. We seemed to have two choices of dying: by our own Allied bombs or at the hands of disenchanted Nazis roaming the area. A third option arose when our planes shot down a German fighter plane which missed us by the smallest of margins.

The last hill to our billet, in what I termed 'a very poor village', was very steep and we all had to struggle to get up it. The billets turned out to be quite spacious which compensated for the fact that the black market appeared to be non-existent although, in fact, I did trade for some yoghurt and a couple of eggs later on. It was not really a problem as our stocks from previous hauls were quite extensive. The official supper comprised boiled potatoes and cold meat, which Reggie and I supplemented with a fry-up of onions and potatoes, washed down with a large cup of Ovaltine – genuine Ovaltine which Reggie had been preserving for a long time.

I did a spot of dab-washing before retiring to bed around 9.30p.m. A combination of three hurried dashes to the bogs, plus incessant bombing and machine gunning in the immediate vicinity, did not give me a restful night. I slept until 8.40 a.m., having been notified the night before that the morrow was going to be another rest day.

DAY 14: **Dittichenrode. Night journey to Wimmelburg**

After early morning ablutions, I decided to have a 'repair and rest' session. The first priority was finding another 'grandmother', which was easier than anticipated, and the rest was routine. I breakfasted on an egg on two slices of fried bread, followed by a potato and onion fry-up. I found Corporal Harry, who was our hairdresser, and got him to give me a 'short back and sides' which restored morale a little. In those days we liked to feel the wind around our necks.

I followed this with another bath in a galvanised iron tub in another farmyard, but, unfortunately no maid-service this time. I even had to do my own laundry, so my first impression of a poor village was turning out to be true. Even the boots and gaiters got a good scrubbing before I settled down to cheese, macaroni and potatoes for lunch. I was so busy, in fact, that I missed church parade: this was completely out of character.

In the afternoon I sat on a bank with Reggie and wrote letters to my family which he promised to deliver if his escape attempt succeeded. After this we stripped off to sun bathe. My back had been aching for the last few days, the weakened back muscles objecting to the load they had to carry for long hours. The sun was really hot for that time of the year, and I saw nothing incongruous in lying starkers face down, whilst our planes hammered targets all round us. Our POW signs were most effective because I cannot recall a single plane giving our party a close inspection. I was not the only one to strip off, so if any plane took photographs, it might have left the WAAF interpreters wondering what we were getting up to.

Our optimism was dealt a body blow when we were told to get ready to move out by truck after dark. Our worst fears looked like being realised because, by the time our little escape syndicate had packed up and met at the rendezvous, it was too late to escape. We had been caught with our pants down: it would have been relatively easy to escape after breakfast, for example, but as soon as the decision to move by road was announced the guard was tightened. We made the most of the hot dinner of meat, onion and potato pie, hoping it would be our last in captivity. We were determined to take the next escape opportunity which arose.

Things did not look any brighter when we were issued with three-fifths of a loaf of bread, followed by another two-fifths. We could read into this that the Germans anticipated a long journey and did not know if, or when, they would be able to feed us again. We went to the senior British officer (SBO) and tried to retract our escape paroles, but he would not accept them. His personal parole was given to cover all ranks under his authority, and there could be no exception to this rule. We did not argue, only reiterating our intentions before walking away. Perhaps not the wisest thing to do, because we were ultimately split up on the journey, which effectively stymied our mass breakout plans. Reggie did not go with us to see the SBO; he saw no point in advertising his intentions, even to the British, and he had formally divorced himself from our syndicate.

We were loaded on the trailers around 9.15p.m. and spent an uneasy period under close guard before moving off at 10.15p.m. We passed through several towns which had received a real pounding from the air. This raised our hopes a little because 'softening-up' on this scale was usually just in advance of the front line. It did not, however, compensate for the fact that escape from the trailer was quite impossible.

Two hours after departure we arrived at a state farm of around 2,000 acres near Wimmelburg, which was originally a monastery. It took an hour to get us settled down into a large barn, which was to be our billet, because there were no lights and we were forbidden to use our fat lamps. I lost contact with Reggie and the others, and, after a fruitless search in the dark, I lay down in the straw just as I was, and fell asleep only to be wakened by rats. One rat actually walked over my face, a nightmare which is still too familiar even now.

CHAPTER 7

The Hazards of Liberty

DAY 15: **Wimmelburg: Reggie goes; Guards disappear**

I did not notice the time when I got up the following morning because Reggie's whereabouts were on my mind. A search for him proved fruitless: I never saw him again – he must have slipped away in the confusion of unloading in the darkness. Later on his discarded bedroll was drawn to my attention so I took possession of it. My family never received the letters he was carrying, so I can only imagine the worst because he was not the sort of man to break a solemn promise. I felt guilty because I had been conducting a successful campaign of emphasizing all problems in escaping, and, the first time I let him out of my sight he jumped camp.

The tragedy of Reggie was that he had endured prison for four years; his decision to go it alone was most unwise and his timing was equally unfortunate because, as later events proved, he would be confronted with the retreating German front line. The real tragedy was that the incarceration, which had become an obsession with him, was literally in the 59th second of the 59th minute of the 11th hour.

There were no ablution facilities available in the part of the farm to which the guards were restricting us, so in the end we moved the cows out of a stall, washed out their trough and filled it with clean water before indulging in what my diary calls a 'cat lick'. I fried an egg for breakfast with great difficulty as the 'goons' were keeping us under close scrutiny. Our escape plans were re-analysed, and we finally accepted that Reggie had succeeded in escaping, only to be dashed when we were told that today was going to be another rest day, and we were all under parole again.

This enabled us to explore the rest of the farm and we sorted out secure hiding places, having made up our minds that this would probably be the last opportunity to jump column.

Rations of jam, honey and cheese were issued, after which I occupied myself boiling up some potatoes to add to the inevitable macaroni and cheese lunch issue. I made contact with some children and 'Dustbin Dan'. In the afternoon I made a potato cake before enjoying some fresh baked scones for tea supplied by the children.

Around 7.30p.m. there was some real excitement when an OP was observed to the south west of us, followed by an artillery barrage at about 6,000 yards range. The shells were landing less than three-quarters of a mile away, which meant that the Allied/German front line could only be a mile away. After the long road journey of the previous night, we had assumed that our forces were miles behind us: the shelling proved just how wrong we were. It did not take our guards long to make up their minds; half-an-hour later, at 8p.m. they all vanished into the night.

Appreciating that we would all have to take turns on guard duty, I decided to try and get some sleep in first, especially as the oil lamps might keep the rats at bay. No such luck! Although I went to bed at 9.05p.m., a tank alarm had us all taking cover at 9.30p.m. Shortly afterwards, the first Allied troops made contact with us: my diary refers to them as Commandos, but in all probability they would have been Rangers.

DAY 16: **Wimmelburg – Sherman tanks**

After this sleep was impossible, even though my official lookout duties only lasted from 4.45a.m. to 5.45a.m.; the next duty roster was at 6.30a.m., so I filled the time in by performing my ablutions. For some reason my duty turn was postponed for an hour, so it was 8.30a.m. on Friday 13 April, that I completed my last official duty in the Oflag.

Around mid-morning our escape syndicate met again, not very enamoured by the order that we were not to leave the confines of the farm. We decided that, although the Allies knew of our existence, so did the Germans, who might drop in a shell to share out amongst us. Our senior officers were walking about the farmyard as though they were in Hyde Park; there were no authorised dispersal points and no orders had been given about how we were to repulse any attempted massacre. The catering had collapsed and all we got were two issues of milk, to which I added my last egg.

Having established that our services as lookouts would not be required again until darkness, we decided to ignore orders and see what was happening outside. All was quiet; a careful recce did not disclose any enemy troops in the immediate vicinity, so we slipped out at the back of the farm and worked our way down the side of the road towards the Allied lines. Approximately half-a-mile from the farm we came across a comfortable looking hollow, shielded from the adjacent road by low bushes. It looked like the sort of place where lovers could achieve privacy in more normal circumstances. We settled down in this hide and arranged our own guard roster: it was very blissful as we took turns in catching up with our sleep.

It was just before noon when we heard the unmistakable sound of approaching tanks. There was a slight dilemma. Was it retreating German armour or ours? I was on 'duty' at the time so it was my responsibility to break cover to establish identity. This was no real problem because, if they were Allied, no one would expect to find a solitary British soldier standing in the middle of the road and, if they were German, we had already worked out our escape route.

I broke cover just after noon, and walked to the centre of the road, just as the lead tank came round the corner masked with trees. I did not need to see the Allied markings to establish its identity, the shape was enough. It was an American Sherman. I moved to the outside of the road waving my outstretched arms above my head; the tank traversed its guns to one side of the road and the following number two tank took the opposite side. I was very conscious of the machine gun in the leading tank pointing straight at me.

The column slowed down to let the lead tank approach me, and an unmistakable Yankee drawl said 'Gee, What's a Brit doing out here?' I quickly filled him in as my two colleagues joined me, telling him where the remainder of the POWs were located and answering his questions regarding German troops. By this time we were all on top of the tank which had resumed its journey towards the farm. We rode back in style, the tank commander wrote his name and address in my diary as he led the attack into Germany, and we shamelessly scrounged food off them. They were most apologetic that they could only give us 'K' rations – to us they were nectar.

The armoured column belonged to 'Old Blood and Guts' General Patton – worshipped by his men and reviled by his fellow generals because of jealousy of his successes. It is interesting to note that another high-ranking British POW shared the same view of this controversial general.

What a display of power! It took four hours for the heavy stuff to pass by, with every vehicle and every man getting a wild enthusiastic reception. The longer-serving POWs could just not comprehend the scale of it all; armies on this scale were not envisaged at the time of Dunkirk. Three tanks were detached to guard our little body of POWs, which gave us a nice feeling of confidence. Having gloated visually over our 'K' ration goodies, we got down to the serious business of eating them.

We held a Thanksgiving Service at 6.30p.m., and heard the English news at 9p.m. before tumbling into bed around 9.45p.m., tired and happy, with a full tummy. Even the three trips to the bogs during the night did not deter me from enjoying a good night's rest, and if the rats were around I was too tired to notice them.

DAY 17: **Wimmelburg – A day on the town**

Saturday, 14 April, dawned nice and bright; I did not wake until 7.45a.m. I had porridge for breakfast to settle my tummy and then went outside to cheer the column which was still passing by, twenty hours after the first tank. It was a leisurely day; the cookhouse was still not yet organised, and the midday meal of curry stew required supplementation with our own supply of peas and potatoes, to which we helped ourselves from the farm stocks.

I expect our senior hierarchy did not have the appropriate army form to requisition peas, etc from the goons! I decided that 'official' meals were not worth waiting for, and in future I would do my own catering. 'Dustbin Dan' turned up again and showed me where all the food stocks were held in the farm. He was brainwashed by years of terrorising and I had to signal to him to help himself. After this I helped to carry his supply to the primitive quarters he had on the other side of the farm – where I found some more of his unfortunate colleagues. They were all Russians whom the Germans tended to look upon as something just above animal status. They were not so deprived as those first slave labour girls we met, but were not far behind. You could tell which were the women, but only just. As soon as I realised how many mouths there were to feed, I took a few of them back for more supplies, carefully taking a circuitous route to avoid the old 'fuddy-duddies' who might not approve of using enemies' food to feed their slaves.

In the afternoon someone organised hot showers in a local factory, after which I enjoyed a substantial meal of cheese and army biscuits. After this a long chat with Wilf and I listened in to the English news again, before meeting up with my old escape syndicate. Like me, they were getting bored with our leisurely lifestyle and we made plans to explore the neighbourhood the following day. This turned out to be very enjoyable; we should have done it much earlier.

To our surprise there were no Americans in the vicinity. Even our three tanks had vanished with the others, over the horizon. One of my companions picked up a Schmeisser automatic. Unfortunately it was not loaded, which is probably why it had been thrown away in the first place. A little further down the road I missed the empty Luger which my other companion spotted before I did. When we walked into the Burgomaster's office to demand the surrender of his town we had two empty weapons to enforce it! Having given him instructions to collect all weapons, cameras, binoculars, etc we retired to an adjacent hotel: we provided the bully beef for the hash which they cooked for us. We were joined by some of our colleagues who had followed us out of the farm.

After lunch we returned to the Town Hall to inspect our haul of weapons, which included a .22 Mauser rifle and, of equal importance, a box of bullets. This was my first choice, followed by two cameras, one with some film in it, and an assortment of Nazi daggers which we stored in our room in the hotel. Four of us then went to the next village to accept its surrender and ran into a bit of excitement. Our arrival prompted the oppressed minority to denounce a Nazi who was hiding in the village. There was a bit of a confrontation outside the Burgomaster's office with half the village wanting us to shoot him out of hand, and the other half wondering if they could rescue him.

The situation was rather tricky until they realised that we were the dreaded British 'fallschirmjagers', after which things quietened down. We went through an elaborate performance of giving custody of the Nazi to the police chief – himself a pro-Nazi, otherwise he would not be holding that post – with a firm assurance that if the prisoner was not handed over to the Allies, when the civilian authority took over from the military he would be shot. I wonder how our Allies sorted that one out. I can just imagine the Police Chief asking for a receipt for his prisoner to avoid getting shot on our return.

Having acquired a few more souvenirs for our collection, we retired to the hotel for a party with two German girls who we had acquired with their young male guitarist. Eggs and potatoes were produced for our supper, together with plenty of beer and a little wine. We had good entertainment from our German hosts who sang their folk songs.

To our starved eyes the two girls looked more attractive than they probably were: when one of them pulled up her skirt to show us a knife wound in her thigh, allegedly inflicted by a Nazi knife,

I realised that the bullet wound in my spine had definitely not severed my sexual drive. After a few weeks in the Oflag I had begun to worry about my wound permanently liquidating any desire for sexual relations. Back in the UK we used to blame this on bromide in the tea but here I sought medical advice. This was most reassuring: 'all due to loss of body tissues, etc, etc,' and 'no improvement until you get on to a proper diet again – nature will soon put that right, when it considers that you have energy to spare'.

I think all seriously wounded prisoners had the same side-effects but the vast majority of them were too embarrassed to ask about it, until I set myself up as a 'family guidance counsellor'. After all, REME was supposed to be the fount of all knowledge.

The doctor was quite accurate in his diagnosis; the scar was very high on the girl's thigh and demanded a close scrutiny – we had been enjoying a more substantial diet over the last two weeks and nature stirred.

All good things must come to an end, and it was with great reluctance that we made our way back to the farm at 7p.m. We had been told that we were moving out at the crack of dawn. I had to repack my kit with the spoils of war before retiring to bed about 9.30p.m. I was far too excited to sleep: we should have stayed longer in the hotel.

DAY 18: **Homeward bound**

I was awake bright and early next morning at 5.30a.m. and breakfasted off eggs and 'K' rations. I washed and shaved before stripping myself of everything that could be of more use to the Russian 'slaves' than my anticipated future needs. I packed it in a blanket, together with stuff others were jettisoning, and took it to the Ruskies – and nearly missed the bus! Since I had last seen them they had captured their old slave master. I gathered he was not a German, so according to my rule book it did not come under the Geneva Convention. Nevertheless, I was a British

The last day in Germany at Wimmelburg

officer, and I was sure that there would be a rule somewhere which said that I must intervene.

The victim was a huge fat slob, in great contrast to his emaciated slave labour force. His great rolls of fat were very noticeable because when I arrived on the scene, he was pegged out on the ground in his birthday suit, with a crude gag in his mouth. The men were standing round in a circle, whilst the girls were, apparently, deciding who should have the pleasure of cutting off the first part with a very rusty knife. He must have been incredibly stupid to stay anywhere in the vicinity of his labour force. I could only assume that he had been caught out by the rapid advance, but if he had any sense he could have disappeared before our guards did.

My popularity with these slaves made me a sort of honorary guru and, to my horror, I found that I was being offered the first slice. The signal from the woman who gave me the knife was quite unmistakable; anything except the penis. It appeared that all the girls had an intimate knowledge of that organ and wanted to reserve that piece of surgery for themselves. In my mind's eye I did not see the Russians gathered around me – all I could feel was the horror of those first slaves in the field near our Oflag – so I declined their generous offer of the first cut, on the grounds that they had pointed out so many detachable souvenirs that death would soon result. My view was that this would be too good and he should be made to suffer some of the deprivations which he had inflicted on them before execution. The women were not very happy about my proposal, but the goodies in the blanket I had brought soon distracted their attention from the old tyrant. He was still in one piece when I hurried back to the convoy of trucks waiting to carry us on the first part of our journey home.

The convoy moved off at 8.25a.m. and passed through Saunderhausen before arriving at Eisenstadt where my group embarked on the ninth Dakota. My last impressions of Germany were mile after mile of fruit trees lining the roadsides, all in glorious blossom, long queues in every town and hamlet, and everyone automatically ducking every time a plane flew

Eisenstadt: Taken with a 'liberated' camera showing the POWs at the airfield

overhead. We crossed the Rhine at 12.30p.m., arriving at Liège at about 1.10p.m., where we lunched off 'K' rations, doughnuts and coffee.

The weather was lovely: this suited our spirits as we walked about a quarter of a mile to wait for an RAF plane to fly us back to the UK. I met some more released POWs including one of my own men who gave me more details of the unit's casualties. We then sat down and waited, and waited, and waited. It turned out to be, in army parlance SNAFU (situation normal: all f****d up). After waiting twelve hours we all crawled into tents, no beds, blankets or even straw to sleep on. I shared Major Milne's groundsheet; the Germans had treated us better than this!

After a most uncomfortable night, we were all up at the crack of dawn. Having given away most of my kit to the Ruskies, assuming the British would be as efficient as the Yanks in backloading us, I had to borrow soap and towel to have a wash. The Yanks must have shared our lack of faith in the RAF turning up, because after breakfasting on more 'K' rations, we were transported to the railway station; I took an extra supply of 'K' rations as emergency rations.

We went by train from Liège to Brussels, where the Red Cross issued us with toilet kits. The officers' shop supplied us with the missing bits and pieces to convert us back into conventional officer's uniform. We were also given white bread, cakes and ice cream in the cafés, free bus transport round the city and real live friendly females to remind us of our loved ones at home.

Obviously, we could not be allowed to enjoy this for too long – SNAFU – after wandering all over Brussels we were recalled for intelligence questioning: but delousing – was that really necessary? We were sent off to bed like small children because of an early start the following morning.

Reveille at 6a.m., was followed by breakfast half-an-hour later and then we were loaded into trucks at 7a.m. – SNAFU again – dismounted from the trucks and we did not leave for a further three-and-a-half hours. More by good luck than providence, we arrived at the airfield to be loaded on to a Stirling from 570

Real girls in Brussels

Squadron, which took off at 12.15p.m. We arrived at Westcote at 1.53p.m. on Wednesday 18 April 1945, to a very warm reception by the WAAFs in a hanger, only spoilt by lurking erks who jumped out to thrust huge nozzles down our trousers and to squirt more lice powder in very intimate areas of our bodies.

After this, no time was wasted in transporting us home: most probably the appropriate bodies in England worked normal hours, whilst those in the fleshpots of Brussels thought that a few hours in the middle of the day were quite adequate. The train clicked its way north; I rushed from the railway station to my parents' house where I had arranged to meet my fiancée. She saw me coming down the avenue and rushed out to meet me, oblivious of the passers-by, and without a word being spoken, we indulged in a long passionate kiss. She pulled her head back, inspected my luxurious moustache, and said these immortal first words to her beloved future husband: 'that's got to come off'.

A very short time later on, I started a happy life sentence in matrimony, so obviously my lucky little fairy who had adopted me on the Arnhem battlefield was still looking after me.

Postscript

Immediately following my return to the UK, my fiancée and I decided to get married. This we did on 19 May 1945, to take full advantage of the six weeks' disembarkation leave given to all returning POWs.

At the compulsory medical examination given to POWs, I was asked the usual questions regarding my wounds, to which I replied that it would be necessary to have the bullet extracted from my spine before I could return to 1st Airborne Division and parachuting.

I was directed to another part of the hospital. I entered the designated door but stopped when I realised what the sign indicated. I stormed back to the first examination room. What I said to the examining doctor was not very polite. He appeared to take little notice of the ravings of an obviously deranged POW, until I said that I knew there was a bullet in my spine because the Germans had X-rayed it. Thinking this was a good way to get rid of me, he gave me a chit for the X-ray Department and an escort of two husky orderlies!

When the plates were developed there was the same reaction in the X-ray Department as there had been in Germany, namely sheer disbelief. As soon as possible I grabbed the plates, ran back and thrust them under the nose of the disbelieving doctor. As you might have guessed, there was no apology and all he said was 'You have no right to be alive!'

The operation to remove the bullet required the services of an outside specialist. It was a long operation, lasting nearly four hours: they could not find the bullet, in spite of taking another X-ray on the operating table. However, I was lucky. As the surgeon started to stitch me up, prior to turning me over to start again from the front, he just caught sight of the bullet tip!

After recovering from the operation, I lay weakly on my bed awaiting the first visit of my brand-new wife. She came in and I waved towards the bullet lying on the bedside table. 'That was the cause of the trouble' I said, waiting with eager anticipation some sympathetic reaction from my beloved. Horror? Nausea? What would be the reaction? All I saw was disappointment.

'What is the matter?' I demanded.

'Nothing', she replied

'Oh! Yes, there is', I responded.

'Well I thought it was bigger than that', she ultimately admitted.

'Bigger! How much bigger?' I asked. She spread her fingers and said 'Well, the ones that I have seen were as big as this'.

The other officers in the ward nearly burst their operating stitches when we realised that she thought the cartridge case was part of the bullet!

Harry Roberts 1990

Afterword

On leaving the forces the author returned to work at the Carriage and Wagon Railway Works in York, the city where he was born. He continued studying and became a Chartered Engineer and a Fellow of the Institute of Mechanical Engineers.

He held numerous senior posts with British Railways, finally becoming the Works Manager of the prestigious Swindon works. He also did consultancy work in Turkey, Egypt and India. Harry had many commitments and interests, one of which was education. He was Chairman of the Governors of several educational establishments in the county. Meanwhile he retained his strong links with REME and the Paras, always attending officers' reunions.

He died suddenly in 1992, aged seventy-one, ending a happy forty-seven year marriage and leaving a family of three sons and a daughter. Harry came from a family of soldiers. His grandfather served in the Boer War and his father was awarded the Military Medal in the First World War and was severely wounded and taken prisoner – history repeated itself.

**The Parachute Regiment
and Airborne Forces prayer**

May the defence of
the Most High
Be above and beneath, around
And within us, in our going out
And our coming in, in our rising
Up and in our going down,
Through all our days and all our
Nights, until the dawn when the
Son of Righteousness shall arise
With healing in His wings for the
Peoples of the world
Through Jesus Christ our Lord

AMEN

Index

Page numbers in italics refer to photographs and maps

Advanced Workshop
 Detachments (AWDs) 10,
 11, 15, 32-3, 35
Air Landing Units 2
air raids
 on forced march 105, 107,
  108, 114-15, 125
 Hanover 58, 62-3
Airborne Division, 1st 1-2,
 18-19
 at Arnhem 17-18, 32-3, 35-8
 disbandment 20
 ésprit-de-corps 2-3
 in Norway 19-20
 officer establishment 4-5
 operations cancelled 11-16
Airborne Division, 6th 3, 11,
 19
ambulance trains 57
Americans 2, 8-9, 47, 129-30
Apeldoorn 48-57
Armoured Division, 7th 12
Arnhem *34*
 battle 14-15, 26-30, 72
 casualty clearing station 30, 32
 Dropping Zones *25*
 landing 24-6
 preparations for 14, 17-18
 REME 18-19, 32-3, 35-8
'Ave Maria' 81

barter 9
bedbugs 61
bicycles 11
black market 89, 93, 104-5, 110,
 117-18
boars 93-4
Brodie, Lieutenant 5, 12, 38
Brooke, Field Marshal Lord 20
Browning pistols 27
Brussels 137

camp concerts 79, *80*
Canadians 77, 102, 120-1
Carrick, Major Jack 1, 2, 5
 Guzzi motorbike 3-4
 leadership 3, 10
 Operation Market Garden
  17
 casualty clearing station 30, 32,
  39, 43-8
chocolate 76

145

Christmas 85, *86*
cigarettes 58–9
Comet 14, 15
condoms 66–7

D-Day 5, 10–12
dandelions 85
Deadman, Captain George 1, 3–4, 5
deafness 84
Diedorf 108–9
Dunlop, Captain 'Dizzy' 3

Eisenstadt 136, *136*
escape committee 94
escape equipment 65, 66
escape plans 118–19, 125–6, 127–9
Evrecy 12
Ewens, Captain F W 5, 17, 33, 35

Fallingbostel 59
film shows 79
food
    as discussion topic 46–7
    K rations 130, 137
    in Oflag 75–9, 85–6
forced march 102, 104–26, *106*
Friedrichsrode 113–14

Gardiner, Private 7–8
generators 97–9
Germans
    Apeldoorn 49, 55–7
    Arnhem 28
    casualty clearing station 44–6, 48

Harz mountains 110–12
Oflag guards 67, 69, 74–5, 82–3, 88, 101–2
Rotenburg 71–2
SS 60, 118, 120–2, 123–4
gliders 2, 12, 17–18
goats 7–8
Gould, Driver 18, 24, 25, 26, 33
Greaves, Craftsman 33
Guzzi motorbikes 3–4

Hackett, Brigadier 'Shan' 1, 3
Hanover 62–3
Hartenstein Hotel 35, *36*
Hayward, Captain R 5, 35
Hicks, Brigadier 'Pip' 2, 3
Hoheneiche 107
Home Guard 13, 27
Hopkinson, General 3
Hotel Vreewijk 30, *31*, 32, 43

ice skating 102
Italy 3–4

jeeps 7, 8

K rations 130, 137
Kinvig, Lieutenant Colonel 5, 17, 33
Kriegie cookers *78*, 79

Lathbury, Brigadier Gerald 1, 3
Lee-Enfield Mk4 27
Leigh-Mallory, Air Chief Marshal 12
Les Andelys 14
Local Defence Volunteers (LDV) 13, 27
lock-picking 95–6

146

Manning, Lieutenant Geoff 5, 10, 12, 17
   Arnhem 32, 33, 35, 38
Market Garden *see* Arnhem
Mascara 2
milk 104, 107
Montgomery, General 2, 12
motorbikes 3–4
M'Saken 2
Mülhausen 110, 111

nettles 85
New Year 85–6
Newby, Captain E G 5
Nohra 115–16
Norway 19–20

Oflag IX A/Z 32, 64, 65–103
Oosterbeek *37*
   Army Casualty Clearing Station 30, *31*, 32, 39, 43–8
   Hartenstein Hotel 35, *36*
Operation Market Garden *see* Arnhem

Parachute Brigades
   1st 1
   4th 1–2, 12
parachute training 2, 9
Paris 14
Patton, General 130
pilferage 7
police liaison 16–17
POW camps
   Oflag IX A/Z 32, 64, 65–103
   Stalag XIB 59, 60–2
POW tools 94, *95*

radios 81, *82*, 97
Raising Brittany 13
Red Cross parcels 77
Reeds, ASM 32, 33
Reggie 110, 114, 123, 124
   escape attempt 121–2, 125, 126, 127
REME *see* Royal Electrical and Mechanical Engineering Corps
Roberts, Harry *vi*, *66*
   Apeldoorn hospital 48–57
   Arnhem 21–5, 27–30
   casualty clearing station 30, 32, 43–8
   forced march 104–26
   Hanover 62–3
   hospital train 57–9
   invasion preparations 13, 14, 17–18
   liberation 127–39
   as police liaison officer 16–17
   postwar career 142
   POW identity card *52*
   SAS 17
   service record xii
   Stalag XIB 60–2
   in training 5–11
   war diary 39, *40–1*, 42, 43
   wound 25–6, 140–1
Roberts, Muriel *66*, 139, 141
roll-calls 81–3
Rotenburg 64, 71–3
   see also Oflag IX A/Z
Rouen 14
Royal Electrical and Mechanical Engineering Corps 1
   at Arnhem 18–19, 32
   reputation 94, 97

147

Royal Electrical and
 Mechanical Engineering
 Corps (*cont.*)
 see also Airborne Division, 1st
Russians
 POWS 62
 slave labour 133, 135

St Malo 13
SAS (Special Air Service) 17
security work 95–101
Sicily 8
skeleton keys 94–5
slave labour 89–92, 115–16,
 131, 133, 135
Sleaford 4
Snow, Captain Hal 1, 5
soap 112
Spangelburg-Kassel 63–4
SS
 fighting units 60
 political 60, 118, 120–2,
  123–4
staff cars 4
Stalag XIB 59, 60–2

Sten guns 27
Sword Hilt 13–14

tanks 12–13
tea 78–9
Titmus, Captain W E 5
tools 94, *95*
Tracy-Bower, Craftsman 18,
 24, 25, 26
Transfigure 14
Turner, AQMS 32, 33

Uthleben 119

water-proofing 5, *6*
Wild Oats 12
Wimmelburg 131–2, *134*
Windeburg 110
wireless 81, *82*, 97
Wolfhaze 30
wood-cutting parties 88–94
workshop trailers, transporting
 5, *6*, 7

X-Rays 73, 140